MW00893602

Hey, Lady
Memoir of a Storyteller
Book 2

By Lynne M. Moore

Author's Note: This book was written from memory and from what records I had available to me. The conversations all come from my recollections and were not written to represent word-for-word transcripts. Rather, I have retold them in a way that evokes the feeling and meaning of what was said. In all instances, the essence of the dialogue is accurate.

Book layout by Linda Hurley
Cover design by Bob Hurley
Original cover artwork by Lynne M. Moore

Acknowledgement

Without the support, advice, and keen perceptions of Linda and Bob Hurley, there would be no book. My gratitude to them for their experience and patience, with profound and heartfelt thanks.

This book is dedicated to Rosemonde Moore Rufin who could have and should have been my mother.

Chapter 1

You know that feeling that something is going to happen? It was mid-summer 1965, when I answered a call from Rob Roberts, a director at the Little Theater where I had worked tirelessly to get the Brandon Little Theatre group established. With the advice and expertise of Sir Francis Goode, actor and director at the Tampa Community Theater, we hoped to build it into a successful cultural resource in Brandon, Florida, by casting amateurs alongside paid professionals.

"Suga," Roberts asked, "can you walk pregnant?"

"Are you kidding, Rob? I've done little else for the past few years."

"Can you come to read the script?" he begged. "I seriously need you. A new guy has the lead in the next play, and the girl chosen to play his wife is too young and she just can't get the walk. Please! I'll have a contract with me."

On that next Monday night, I encountered Bob DuMouchel for the first time. Upon entering the darkened rehearsal hall, I was greeted by a booming voice as I stepped into the light. "Hey, Blondie," the voice said, "are you gonna be my next wife?"

My initial impression of DuMouchel was that of a middle-aged man with stunning blue eyes, high cheekbones, a masterful physique, and the stink of cigarettes. I was told that he had moved his family to Mango, just a few miles from Brandon.

I was doubtful that we could keep him when I learned of his impressive bio; we were unaccustomed to having such an experienced actor in our midst. His credits included "Guys and Dolls" and "The Desperate Hours" with the American Theater Guild in Canada; "Finian's Rainbow" with the Newfoundland Theater Guild; and "The Merchant of Venice" and "Time Out for Ginger" with the Grand Rapids Civic Theater in Michigan. He had also trodden the boards of many stages during his twenty years in the Army, while singing with the USO. And, he was just ending a stint with the touring company of "Paint Your Wagon," singing the lead role of Ben Rumson.

Despite the fourteen years difference in our ages, over the next few years and a variety of acting roles, Bob and I proved to work well together. I was cast as his wife, his daughter, his enemy, his lover, his co-conspirator, and his jailer in six successful productions. We both came away with enough rewards and honors to paper our walls.

From our first encounter, chemistry on stage was immediately evident. Later, his wife, June, told me that many actors found him difficult to work with because he refused to rehearse seriously. Did I let Bob DuMouchel intimidate me? Not on your life! I gave it right back, in theatrical parlance, "threading the needle." If he said one of my lines, I responded with his! If he adlibbed, so did I, and the audience never suspected. We worked magic together and it became a game we relished for the next few seasons. Coincidentally, one of his heroes was Rex Harrison, whose reputation in theatre circles named him a gifted provocateur, who endlessly played pranks on fellow cast mates while maintaining a straight face.

June encouraged directors to cast me opposite her husband when other actresses refused to risk appearing with a man of his vast experience and reputation.

When my husband, Jim, was on the road, I took my six children to rehearsals, where they joined the six DuMouchel kids; the twelve ranging in ages from five through fifteen. June would ride herd over all twelve in the theater lobby, where she made them do their homework and kept the preschoolers occupied. Sometimes she would usher all of them quietly into the darkened theater to watch the action on stage. They sat engrossed through endless rehearsals and often learned the actors' lines before they did.

It wasn't long before many of the kids were selected to perform. Commercial directors called upon our two families, knowing we could provide almost any age child with stage discipline and some experience. The kids joyfully pitched right in, rehearsed tirelessly and developed a repartee beyond their years. June and I were not above dying little heads or using wigs to fit the requirements of any role. Soon, some had their own Screen Actors Guild (SAG) memberships and were earning some money, too.

I had been given the same opportunity as a child. My mother, Germaine Moore, worked for a company that hired me and my brother, Jerry, when we were only 9 and 8, respectively, for commercials that played in movie theaters. Our bits played before and after the feature, much the way popcorn, soda and "stifle your cell phone" are promoted today. Because we earned money, we had to obtain Social Security cards and joined SAG and AFTRA (American Federation of Television and Radio Artists).

The nun in charge of the theatrical program at my elementary school, Holy Rosary, had a connection with a professional theatre in the French Quarter, Le Petite Theatre du Nouvelle Orleans. When the director requested a female child, small for her age, but with the mental capacity of an older child, the sister agreed that I could handle it. I had been in elocution class since kindergarten and was not timid. My benefactor, granddad Pierre Sarrat, who had loved attending the theater as a young man, was intrigued and allowed me to miss as much school as required to take on a role. His chauffer, Tomas, delivered me and waited patiently through three weeks of rehearsals and three more of performances. I was paid ninety dollars that went straight into my bank.

Through my high school years, I also performed in a weekly radio drama. I was overheard saying, "My name is Catherine Warren," in my sleep. Those were my opening words on the radio show, voiced standing on a box to reach the mike at WSMB. Also, any time our drama club performed a play, I was right there. I was honored with the Thalian Award for three consecutive years during that time. My grandad encouraged me by paying my dues to AFTRA, to maintain my professional status.

Suga's early stage career

Despite my early successes in the theater, acting was not my dream. I wanted to become an artist and designer. However, after marrying Jim Mouton in 1956, I found myself willing, and actually thrilled, to give up any silly dream of a career and just be the best wife and mother I could be. My six babies were born in seven years, so I had my hands full. Besides, I soon had all the drama, in my daily life, that I could handle.

Chapter 2

I had learned of Jim's first "slip" back in 1959, just three years after our marriage. I sought counselling from our parish priest who advised me: "You can forgive him, but you'll never be able to forget it. I want you to promise me that you won't bring it up or use it against him." So, although he continued cheating on me over the years, I took it on the chin, neither discussing his indiscretions nor berating him for his affairs.

Ten years later, Jim used my silence as his reason for getting a divorce. It seems that my refusal to rant and rave over his infidelities caused him to be guilt-ridden and he couldn't face me anymore. Frankly, after years of separation while traveling for work, Jim had emotionally weaned himself from the children and me.

Although we agreed to keep up the semblance of a relationship for the children, I knew it was only a matter of time before he would either want to remarry or be forced into it by one of his paramours. At that point, my financial support would be, at the least, greatly diminished, if not gone all together.

With no college education or substantive work experience, I would have to find a way to support myself and the children. For many years, I had taken in sewing and taught ballroom dancing at country clubs or school auditoriums (trained by Arthur Murray Dance Studio), wherever we lived. Would that be enough to pay the mortgage, doctors, and put food on the table? Not likely.

When we married, I was an over-indulged 20-year old with a mind of her own and no practical experience. Babies had come in rapid succession and I was committed to keeping them safe, well dressed and fed, while following Jim from New Orleans to Texas to Alabama to Arkansas, back to New Orleans, and then to Georgia and Florida. All these moves came in the space of eight years.

I struggled with my sense of loss and helplessness and invoked the Blessed Mother's help daily. I was a good Catholic girl who depended on her spiritual mother and I would continue to credit her with my successes throughout my life and call on her for support during trying times. Despite my inner fears and turmoil, I attempted to keep things as normal as possible. The children were confused, but accepted Jim's erratic visits. And why not? He had spent all our married life on the road except for the year he had worked for W.T. Grant as an assistant manager in Houston.

The uncertainty of our situation once again raised abandonment issues in me. Mignon and Pierre Sarrat, my benefactors, had taken me in as a "grandchild" when, as a newborn, I was left at a hospital in New Orleans. Their eldest daughter, Germaine, had left a note bearing their phone number, pinned to my blanket, and then walked away. The Sarrats were already responsible for fifteen children; their own seven, plus eight nieces and nephews orphaned by the deaths of both Mignon's sister and brother-in-law. Then they accepted me, with no proof that I was their grandchild. Christened Lynne Marie, I was nicknamed "Suga." Amelia, my old "Mammy," who spoke not a word of English, called me "Sucre," the French word for sugar, but she didn't know how to spell it in English. When I was ready to start school, she felt obliged to teach me to write my name, and this was the result. I maintain it in her memory.

As the story goes, Germaine had enticed Bruce Moore, a handsome playboy from another prominent family, into impregnating her. It was widely held by the Sarrat family that this was only done so that "wild" Germaine could escape her mother's control. However, to complicate matters, Rose Moore, Bruce's sister, was also pregnant and unmarried, at the same time. Both girls were sent out of town to stay with a midwife to avoid scandal. The story that the girls told was that they were sedated and when they awoke were told by the midwife that only one child survived. The midwife then had the girls draw straws and in Germaine's own words, she "got stuck" with me.

In hindsight, the story was not so much a tale with a beginning, middle and ending, as it was whispered fragments and inuendo woven together over the years until, in my mind, it was whole cloth.

It's like some fractured fairytale. Two dear friends get pregnant at the same time, neither having a partner with the gumption or desire to stand up. Then they are sent away together and seemingly go into simultaneous labor, are sedated, and wake up to find there is only one baby. And the midwife's solution is to have the girls draw straws? What would have been her motivation in withholding the identity of the surviving child? And, if my mother truly didn't want me, why not give me to Aunt Rosie, her best friend, who sincerely wanted a child?

Unfortunately, I will never know the truth. My mother stuck to her story until the end. It has taken me many years to reconcile myself to the fact that it no longer matters.

Bruce would later say that he had bickered with Germaine for years because she refused to reclaim me from her parents. Perhaps that was true. Who knows? They later had two boys, whom they kept. Bruce spent his career in the Army, therefore I saw little of him until I was grown. They would float in and out of New Orleans, visiting their families between duty stations, but they always left me behind.

I never asked why. I could speculate that Mignon stood in my parents' way out of spite; or perhaps she even provided a monetary incentive to keep them on the periphery of my life. Certainly, a more palatable excuse than that they just didn't want me. I have added this to my list of things that just don't matter anymore.

Throughout my childhood, the Sarrats provided me with a beautiful home, a personal maid, an education and other comforts. Their generosity was astounding. However, I was repeatedly admonished by Mignon to be grateful to her because she took me in when nobody wanted me, a point she felt obligated to repeat, ad nauseam, which colored my life for decades.

As my marriage deteriorated, so did my mental and physical health. I was losing weight and my concentration grew feeble. I went to bed most nights with my rosary in my hand. All night I lay alone in the dark, my eyes wide open. This was my personal problem, I couldn't call my mother or a friend in the middle of the night. What could they possibly say? Who cared? And I had to keep Jim's secrets. No one must know he was a cheat. Often, I sank into unending confusion, like a kite broken free of its string.

Chapter 3

My involvement with the Brandon Little Theatre brought me to my feet and out of the house for the next year. A neighboring theatrical club, "The Villagers", approached us suggesting a merger of the two groups. They were schoolteachers who staged plays in their auditoriums for their own entertainment, but we saw a wealth of talent and enthusiasm that could add an important dimension to our theatrical community. There were, of course, legal ramifications, the requisite new designs for our programs, and the need for lots of publicity. Ultimately, we emerged a larger, livelier group called "The Village Players," and I was elected president.

Jim became interested, and joining our board of directors, contributed his business acumen. Coupled with Bob Du-Mouchel's stage experience, we evolved as a major voice in the Florida Theater Conference. The most surprising development was Jim's willing participation in an actual play. He and Bob began rehearsals for "Mary, Mary" and when Germaine and Bruce rolled into town in their Airstream, they conned my father into playing a cameo role.

While the children enjoyed having their grandparents parked in our driveway, this proximity also gave them a front row seat to the saga of our failing marriage. After a month of their well-meant advice, I had to ask them to move to a nearby trailer park. Divorce is simply neither a team nor an exhibition sport.

Bob had been down with pneumonia and the new director, James LaRue, was frantic to cast a strong male lead for the opening play of the 1968-69 theater season, "Bell, Book and Candle." As president, I went out to Bob's house, hoping to persuade him to make a comeback, if he was well enough. He wouldn't be doing it for me, he was a sucker for applause, as all of us are on the stage. You must be a certified egomaniac to put in so much work for the pittance the regional theaters pay!

Apparently, I was persuasive enough and DuMouchel pulled us out of a tight spot when he agreed to read for the part. There were several women in the cast and crew who put themselves in his way any chance they got, but to no avail. While he was attractive and dynamic, what these women soon realized was that Bob was not a ladies' man. He still saw June as twenty-five, youthful, and beautiful. He simply showed no interest in other women.

In high school, Bob had been a Golden Gloves contender with little time for girls, so he left no broken hearts when he volunteered for military service. From Michigan, he was sent to Camp Claiborne, Louisiana, then on to Ft. Riley, Kansas, for cavalry training, still on horseback in those days. Later, Bob was among the selected few to go to Aberdeen Proving Ground in Maryland, where he joined the mechanized cavalry and was taught to operate tanks. Promotions came fast when the 1st Infantry Division was sent to the North Africa invasion. Bob made sergeant at nineteen and was given a platoon of thirty-two men. He landed in Normandy the day after D-Day, then went into reconnaissance and finally joined the 7th Army north of Marseilles. The Germans captured him and his last five men near Strasbourg. After three grueling months in a POW camp near Munich, Bob, another sergeant and a gutsy major walked away from a road detail. Not daring to look back, they made their way to their own lines, with great difficulty; considering themselves luckier than most.

Less than two weeks later, he climbed into a tank and was the only survivor when it hit a landmine. The explosion propelled his body up into the turret, face first, smashing his jaw, destroying his teeth, and breaking every bone from his shoulder to his left hip, plus both legs. He crawled into a ditch and lay there until the medics found him.

After being placed in a mammoth body cast in a field hospital in Nancy, France, he was flown to a general hospital in England. With only his right arm free, Sergeant DuMouchel became a terror to the nurses, who quickly learned to feed him and administer to his needs from his harmless left side. Eventually, after being fitted with a new set of teeth and a smaller body cast to accommodate his significant weight loss, he was sent back to the States for thirteen months of mending at Percy Jones Hospital in Michigan.

Glen Lindsey occupied the next bed, and his sister, June, visited regularly. During one of her visits, June confided to her brother that Bob DuMouchel was the man she was going to marry. On September 6, 1946, they were married at St. Francis Xavier Church in Grand Rapids, Michigan, with his brother and her sister as witnesses, and only their parents in attendance.

Bob and June

June's career as a legal secretary came to an abrupt halt when Michael was born. Bob reenlisted, this time in the Air Force. He said, "A man could get hurt playing with guns down on the ground." He knew from experience.

They were stationed in Okinawa, where native houseboys took good care of the 'Honcho' and his family. His rugged good looks and easy smile charmed the little people. By the time they returned to the states, June was pregnant with Steve. The next tour of duty took them to Germany, and then Lincoln, Nebraska, where they were posted long enough for June to deliver two more boys, Danny and Pat. It seemed a beautiful surprise named Kathryn Marie would complete their family, or so they thought, until Jeffrey was born while they were stationed in Newfoundland.

"I'm going to retire at the end of this month, Bob," the commander told his right-hand man and confidant of seven years, now Sergeant Major DuMouchel.

"Well, sir," Bob replied, "I've put in twenty-two years myself, so I'll retire when you do. It would take me too long to break in another general."

Upon retirement, Bob weighed seriously the financial risk of going exclusively on the professional stage opposed to his duty to provide a stable income for his family. The stage had been an avocation all these years; he sang in clubs and performed in theaters all over the world, becoming a member of AFTRA which afforded him union scale for his appearances. The decision was ultimately made when a doctor diagnosed June's excessive weight loss as cancer. Their move to Florida was for the specific purpose of filling the remainder of her life with warmth and sunshine. Regional theatre would have to suffice.

Chapter 4

In early November 1968, following the final performance of "Bell, Book and Candle," June came to the cast party looking healthier than she had in years, though still thin as a rail. Her hair was nicely done, and she wore a good-looking beige suit. She was in a great mood. We giggled in the ladies' room, oblivious to the banging on the door, while she helped me struggle out of an uncomfortable girdle and remove my pantyhose. We then dodged and weaved through the boisterous, jam-packed crowd as we held each other up, laughing helplessly. We ignored everyone who tried to talk to us, concealing my contraband through the crowded party to deposit my unmentionables in my car. Although we had grown very close over the intervening years, she was not forthcoming about her precise medical condition. What I didn't know was that she had leukemia and a weak heart.

The following Sunday, Jim had made his usual token appearance at church with the children and me. He was a leader in the Boy Scouts in our parish and president of the PTA, so we spent the afternoon at the annual church fair, carrying out our farce of a happy marriage. He was living in a rented trailer when he wasn't on the road, but no one on our street suspected. After the inevitable barbecued chicken and coleslaw, we drove home in silence while the children raved about the marvels they had seen in the tacky fair booths. When all six were bathed and bedded down, Jim assembled his briefcase and prepared to leave, but was interrupted when the phone rang at about 10 p.m. It was Bob.

"Jim, can I come over? I know it's late, but I need to see you."

"Sure, Bob, we're up." A few minutes later the bell rang, and Jim let an ashen-faced DuMouchel into the living room.

"You look awful, pal, did something happen?" Jim inquired.

"I came to ask you to be a pallbearer, Jim." Bob hesitated, and his eyes filled up. "June died tonight on the way to the hospital."

"Oh, no!" Jim was shocked. "I'm so sorry." He turned to the bar and poured Bob a drink. "What happened?"

"I haven't been home to tell the kids yet. I guess I'm putting it off as long as I can. June had chest pains for an hour or so this afternoon. I called a doctor, but he wouldn't make a house call 'cause she wasn't his patient. So, I headed for MacDill, a habit I guess, after my years in the service."

"We had just turned on to Bayshore Drive when she stiffened up and begged me to please not let her die! She was only 44 years old! We knew she had leukemia, but it was too soon! When we got to MacDill, I jumped out of the car and ran into the ER, callin' for a medic, and they responded immediately. But it was too late." He started to sob. "She's gone, Jim! We came to Florida, so she could die in a warm place. She couldn't even go outside in Michigan."

"Is there anyone we can call for you?" Jim asked.

"No. I'll call our families after I wake the kids up and tell them. I don't want anyone phonin' my house before they know."

I spoke up, "Bob, it's not my place to tell you what to do, but please wait until the kids wake up in the morning and tell them then." It was the best advice I could offer.

"You're right, Lynne. Thank you."

"Jim, can I count on you to get the rest of the pallbearers for me? I don't want my boys to have to do it." Bob had five sons, only two of whom were teenagers. It was his call. Jim and I, temporarily, put aside our personal problems to help him.

Our friends in the theater rallied around Bob and his parents drove over from Sarasota to help guide the silent, stunned children to their seats for their mother's funeral.

The chapel was packed with friends Bob didn't realize he had. I sat dumbfounded; we had never had a friend die and I couldn't accept that it had really happened. June and I had been laughing together just a week ago. The priest's voice brought me back to the present. The fragrance of flowers permeated the walls at the saddest funeral I had ever seen.

For months afterwards, a somber quiet hung over the Du-Mouchels' little pink, cement-block house. Grief and depression seemed to settle on the place like a heavy fog, blocking out the view. Bob refused to go back into their master bedroom and with manic strength and determination, removed a wall, thereby enlarging the living room and eradicating it. Now, with no bedroom of his own, he sat on the sofa all night, the television droning endlessly. Most nights he cried until exhaustion took over and then stretched out, fully clothed, for a few hours of restless sleep.

He spent his days alternately sitting under the pines at the cemetery staring at June's grave and hovering over his family. Irrationally, he believed that his children would also be snatched away from him unless he kept them in his sight. He kept them from attending school, until a truant officer forced him to allow them to return. He gave up his job cutting grass on a golf course, and spent his time doing housework, mopping and polishing terrazzo floors and cooking for the children. November blended into December, but he seemed to have no sense of time passing.

The night before her mother died, ten-year-old Kathy had argued with her; voices were raised and without realizing the gravity of her words, Kathy shouted, "I wish you were dead!" The child was so shocked by her mother's subsequent death that she stopped speaking all together for months.

The Junior Women's Club in Brandon put the DuMouchel family on their charitable list and asked me to deliver Christmas gifts.

"Hey, lady!" Jeff, the youngest boy, was out in the yard when I pulled up and he spied the gift boxes. "Dad, Dad! That lady's here," he ran screaming toward the house.

"Whadaya say, hon!" Bob greeted me at the door. "You haven't been around much. Is Jim with you?" He looked over my shoulder toward my car.

"Jim and I are separated, Bob," I said bluntly. I wanted to bite my tongue. He didn't need to be burdened with my problems.

"I'm sorry," he said sympathetically. "I thought something was wrong between the two of you. I wouldn't have told a soul, but I've seen Jim here and there. I thought he might be runnin' around on you."

"No secret anymore. There's nothing official, maybe we'll work it out," I said.

"Is it that skinny brunette? I hear she's bad news."

"Probably. I don't know this time, but we agreed to separate so we could catch our breath."

"Is there anything I can do? Would you like me to talk to him?"

"No, you have enough on your mind. How are the kids?"

"They miss June. It's hardest on the little ones, Jeff and Kathy. I take them over to my folks' place in Sarasota on weekends to keep 'em busy, get 'em out of the house. Mike and Steve are comin' back from Michigan where they were visitin' June's family. Say, why don't you bring your boys over some afternoon? Dan and Pat have a football game goin' every evening in the lot next door. They're even lettin' Kathy play, and she runs away with the game because they won't tackle her like they do each other. Maybe Eddie and Peter need a break from their sisters."

I thanked him for the suggestion and told him I would mention it to the boys. I left the Christmas gifts and went home, profoundly sorry for Bob and his family.

Chapter 5

Germaine and Bruce had been touring in their Airstream trailer since his retirement and made a stop to see the kids and me on the day before my thirty-third birthday. I cried in my mother's arms for the first time in my life. She poured coffee while I outlined my plan to save Jim from the grips of his latest girlfriend.

"He wants a divorce," I said, "but I believe if I refuse, he'll drop her and eventually come home."

Dad berated me. "Suga, you don't have the right to decide what Jim is doing with his life. Someday it will suit you to be free, too. You can't play God."

They only stayed overnight before heading north to look at boats. Dad, having powered first his father's yacht, "Wendy", then armored ships during the war, was now planning to build his own Ferro Cement, fifty-four-foot, oceangoing ketch.

Later, Jim came by to pick up the kids, although I had begged him not to, hoping to avoid spending my birthday alone. The kids and I had been an inviolable team long before their father left us, and I needed them. I stood with knees of jelly as a part of my heart came unfastened.

"Sorry," he said, "I have tickets to a rodeo tomorrow, and they'll have a great time." I felt like a child myself, inadequate to the task of convincing him. I knew the children would have a good time, so I faced a long, lonely weekend, feeling sorry for myself.

I kissed them all goodbye and slowly got into my car as his disappeared around the corner. I was going to my friend Betsye Gorman's house to borrow one of her albums after I had picked up a few things at the grocery for my birthday dinner. Coming out of the store I nearly collided with Bob.

"Hi, Bob," I said with a long face.

"Hey, good to see you. What are you up to?"

"Just a bit of shopping." I don't know what possessed me, but I found myself saying "I'm going to listen to a recording of Man of La Mancha tonight, would you like to join me? It's my birthday. Jim took the kids and I have a jug of homemade wine and some cheese. If you're interested, I'll share it with you."

"Sure, what time?" He said, without hesitation.

"Make it about twenty hundred hours," I said, showing off my knowledge of military lingo. That would give me time to straighten up my living room.

I was strangely nervous as I bathed and dressed. I wasn't in the habit of entertaining without Jim. What would I say when Bob came? What if he didn't come? I sat and wrung my hands. What if he was bored listening to a whole album alone with me? What an absurd thing for me to have done, inviting him over to listen to records! He must think I'm an adolescent fool.

At eight o'clock sharp the doorbell rang, and I deliberately slowed my pace as I approached the foyer and opened the door. There stood Bob, impeccably dressed in a dark suit and tie. After we exchanged awkward greetings and he was inside, he grinned sheepishly as he extended the two gift boxes he had concealed behind his back.

"Am I the first one here?" he asked, looking around me.

"Oh, Bob, I'm sorry. Did I give you the impression I was having a party? I just borrowed a fantastic album from Betsye and I didn't want to be alone on my birthday," I apologized.

He mumbled something as I opened the gifts and thanked him. One was a box of candy, the other a pair of tiny, delicate pierced earrings. How observant of him to notice my ears were pierced! Not one man in a hundred pays attention to such things. I brought out my home-brewed wine and handed him two glasses.

The records were on the turntable and thankfully gave our stilted conversation relief as we became engrossed in Don Quixote, Sancho and Aldonza.

"Nice," Bob commented as he sipped the wine and snuffed out his third cigarette. He was as nervous as I was.

"Yes, it's a great album. Have you seen the play? Or read the script? Do you want more wine?" I offered.

He cleared his throat before answering, "No, yes, it's heavy, thank you."

"The wine?" I asked.

"The play. Kylie plays it light, but it's a deep, moving story," he explained.

"I don't understand it."

"The play?" he asked.

"The wine. Sometimes it's bad, sometimes it's good. I try to make it the same way each time. This batch must have quite a high alcohol content, I feel giddy," I confessed.

He went on with his explanation of the story. "The Lord of La Mancha, Don Quixote, and the Knight of the Woeful Countenance are the same, don't you see? He's imprisoned durin' the French Inquisition and is tryin' to vindicate himself before the other prisoners. He hasn't had his real trial yet, it's a play within a play, you see."

"But where is the inn supposed to be? And who is Sancho? Dulcinea and Aldonza, are they two women or one? The voices sound the same. Why would he want to fight a windmill? Do you want some more wine?" I was babbling.

"Whew, you don't make it easy," he sighed.

"Oh, yes, it's easy, but it takes eight weeks to make. It's simply a matter of mixing grape juice with sugar, yeast, and water in a big crock and waiting for it to ferment."

"The wine?" he said with a grin.

"Of course, the wine, what did you think I was talking about?"

"I don't know, and I don't think you know either. Are you all right?"

"All right!" I was indignant and got up unsteadily to turn over the records, but the stereo kept getting farther and farther away as I attempted to cross the room. After I had the stack of 78's in my hands, I couldn't find the little hole. Suddenly, Bob was beside me.

"I'll do that. You go back and sit down." He gently kissed me on the cheek.

"Did you invite me here to compromise me?" I asked teasingly.

"I didn't invite you here at all, this is your house. You invited me here to listen to this album, and I'm doin' just that." He led me back to the sofa and sat holding one of my hands in both of his. "Don't you think you've had enough of that wine?"

"Certainly not. Do you think I'm drunk? Please pour me another glass."

"All right, but after this one, I'm goin' home."

I gulped my wine. "You can't go home, you came to hear the album. This is my birthday, please don't go yet, I love you!" I blurted.

"That was the second time we've turned those records over and its nearly midnight. Happy Birthday. And you don't love me, you're just lonely and so am I. That's why I'm goin' home." He kissed me on the cheek again. I felt weak. "You and I have been friends for a long time and you're startin' to look awfully good to me." He headed for the door.

"Bob," I started after him, "thank you for the candy and the earrings."

"Goodnight," he said, and he was gone.

Sunday morning, I dragged myself out of bed and straight to the Alka-Seltzer. I dressed for mass, wearing a chapel veil over my throbbing head instead of a hat, and went to Nativity Church alone. I arrived home an hour later, and without meaning to, I slammed the car door and nearly keeled over from the impact it had on my headache.

My friend, Jo Ann Shearn, was coming out of her mother's house across the street and I suddenly remembered that we had planned to sit down that afternoon to make final decisions about the design of her wedding dress. She must have seen my anguish, because as she crossed the street she made 'tch-tch-tch-tch' noises. I told her about my birthday guest.

"Now you watch that, Lynne," she said with a wink. "You'd better call me to chaperone next time you have company or people will talk."

"There won't be a next time, Jo Ann," I said sadly. "I really blew it."

"Oh, now…" she started, but I gripped her arm as I stared down the street. Bob's gray Plymouth was turning into my subdivision. It was difficult to conceal my pleasure as he pulled into my driveway and got out. I was glad I hadn't changed from my Sunday pink linen, and suddenly, my head didn't hurt anymore. He nodded to Jo Ann and addressed me.

"I just left my laundry at the laundromat and have a few minutes to kill. I thought I should come by to see how you are."

"Wonderful," I answered, "would you like to come in and have lunch and something cold to drink?"

"No thank you to lunch. I have to go home and feed my kids. Maybe something cold to drink, but please, no wine," he said smiling.

Jo Ann made a pitcher of lime Kool Aid and we all sat on the porch. With no mention of my foolish declaration of the previous night, we discussed the characterization and theory behind "Man of La Mancha." I had to fake a lot, because I couldn't remember all I'd heard, and I had understood only half of that. Jo Ann got bored and was just about to leave when Jim brought the children home, much earlier than usual. His girlfriend wasn't with him for a change.

The kids seemed to explode from the car in every direction, all talking at once, each trying to claim my attention.

"Say hello to Mr. DuMouchel," I admonished them.

"Hello, Mr. Boomershell," Missy and Suzi, my babies, chorused. The others handled it somewhat better.

"Hi, Bob, good to see you," Jim offered his hand. They exchanged a few words, then each headed for his own car and left, while I stood by like a cigar store Indian.

"I'll be over one day to clean the rain gutters and cut the grass," Jim called as he pulled away. Sure he would, in my dreams.

I cut the grass myself Monday morning. Then at noon, Bob surprised me when he showed up in work clothes and offered to clean the gutters.

"Who's the man outside on the ladder?" Nellie, my housekeeper, asked.

"That's Mr. DuMouchel, Nellie. You remember, he lost his wife last winter and he's taking care of his children all by himself. Let's whip up a cake for him to take to them."

"Don't he have six children and a house of his own?" Nellie asked. "And he's out here doin' all this for you? Ain't he a nice man?" she continued, slyly.

"Cake, Nellie, just bake him a cake and get that gleam out of your eye."

"Yes, Ma'am."

The neighbors and our friends were shocked when my divorce filing came out in the papers. Betsye was hurt. "Why didn't you say anything?" she asked over coffee on my porch.

"Because, Betsye, he's president of the PTA, assistant scout master, and a hotshot salesman. Should I let on that he's also an adulterer? We have a reputation to uphold. Anyway, who would believe it of Mr. Congeniality?"

"You could have told me." She pretended to pout.

"No, I couldn't. I know how much you think of him. Now, I have to smile at everyone at church when I know they're wondering what I did to make him leave."

"What did you do?" Betsye's eyes got big, as her eyebrows raised.

"I did nothing, except quietly put up with his philandering. For thirteen years I kept my mouth shut about his affairs! Then he says, I made him feel guilty because I didn't harp about it. He has agreed to go to counseling, but I don't believe he will change. His girlfriend even had the nerve to call and ask me to file for the divorce. But I'm not going to let him off that easy. If he wants it, he can file. And, let's not forget, Florida has "no fault" divorce, so not even the state will hold him accountable."

"Explain to me," Betsye wanted to know, "why someone as smart as you put up with his cheating for **thirteen years**."

"I thought if I were patient enough, he'd remember that he loved me. Not to mention that I have no education and six children who need a peaceful home. Oh yes, and Catholics don't get divorced!"

Chapter 6

"Mr. DuMouchel's here, Mama." Leslie roused me from a troubled sleep, one Saturday morning. I told her to explain to Mr. DuMouchel that I was unfit to receive company, miserable with a temperature and a hacking cough. But Bob remained, undaunted.

I relented, crawling out of bed to flop into an easy chair in the sunny living room, disheveled and feeling wrung out. I asked him to bring a pitcher of lemonade and glasses. Realizing I was too sick to do it, he rounded up the children and fed them lunch, adding to my meager supplies some of the goodies he had just bought for his kids. Having taken on the role of both mother and father in his home, he was tuned in to what was needed. I was struck by his comfort level with them and the way they responded to him.

After a few days' rest, I was well enough to attend my weekly bridge game, and afterwards decided to visit Bob. I found him in his living room, watching TV surrounded by his four younger children and bowls of popcorn. His two oldest boys, Mike and Steve, were back home from visiting June's sister in Michigan and there was a marked difference in his spirits. He was almost jovial.

As I joined them, five-year-old Jeff curled up beside me on the sofa, snuggling up to the mink collar on my coat. He had still not learned my name, "Hey, lady," he said, "this is soft." He petted it like a kitten.

I told him about smearing peanut butter on the mink once when Missy got chewing gum on it. "Peanut butter..." he repeated while he buried his face in the fur. In a few minutes, he was asleep.

The kitchen door banged, steps sounded, and a young man appeared in the doorway. I hadn't seen Steve, now 16, since he was young. He looked over my black crepe dress, adorned with a single strand of pearls, and took in my carefully coiffed French twist. I received what appeared to be an expression of mild approval. He was not as tall as Mike, his older brother, but had broader shoulders and slim hips encased in tight jeans, a cigarette in his right hand. He was an extremely handsome boy, much like his father, but with darker, mid-length wavy hair. He had come to tell his dad that he had landed a job with the local veterinarian, Dr. DeRing.

And so, over the next few months, our lives fell into a comfortable rhythm. Our two families often sat together at little league games, attended church as a group, and shared picnic suppers regularly. Mike and Steve refereed the backyard family football games when they were available, but were, naturally busy with their own friends.

I was intrigued by Bob's teenagers. Having only younger children, I had to rely on what I'd heard; that all young people were sitting around smoking pot, sniffing glue, or getting high on LSD. I soon learned that my conception of the generation was sadly inaccurate, when, a month later, I asked them privately, if they could get me some pot from their hippie friends.

"Don't take this unless I'm with you," Mike said, as he slipped a capsule into my hand in the darkened theater. We had loaded the kids into two cars and taken them to Tampa Community Theater to see Steve perform in a drama competition for a scholarship. Before he went on stage, he also made his way to my aisle seat.

"Dad will kill me for this, but here!" And Steve thrust something into my hand. It felt similar to what Mike had given me.

Bob changed places with Missy and was now sitting next to me as Steve was being introduced. "The boys told me about your problem," Bob whispered. I froze. He extended his closed hand to me, and when I opened mine to accept what his contained, he deposited a third capsule! "Don't take it unless I'm with you."

I was mid-thought, trying to decide if I had blundered into a family of drug pushers when I finally looked at what I held. They weren't drugs at all, but oversized glycerin suppositories for dogs. I imagine Steve and Dr. DeRing had quite a laugh at my expense.

On stage, Steve's monologue was excellent. He delivered a dramatic scene from "Peace is an Olive Color," and all of Mark Twain's, "The Golden Arm." He was easily selected for the finals. Then the director, Francis Goode, whom I knew well and had worked under several times, called me aside as we were herding the children out.

"Now I expect Steve to win this scholarship, Ducky," he said in his best Queen's English. "How many more are there?"

"How many more what, Francis?" I was perplexed.

"Younger children," he said.

"Steve is the second, there are four more, but I don't know if the others are interested in a career in theater."

"All together how many?" he insisted, gesturing to the entire group.

"Between us? Twelve, but the oldest is nearly 18…"

"So, I have to get scholarships for ten DuMouchel children! You'll hardly be able to send them all to college on your own," he stated emphatically.

To avoid "dating", which seemed ludicrous at our stage in life, Bob and I attended many theater-related functions together. On the infrequent occasions I was asked out by other gentlemen, I began finding reasons why I wasn't available.

In time, we became each other's helpmates; he changed the oil in my car and did repair chores around my house, and I shopped for his children's school supplies and occasionally mended their clothes. To supplement a meager Air Force pension, Bob tossed pizzas at a shop next door to the Brandon movie theater.

Occasionally, when he and his family were out, I went to Mango and put a frozen dish in his freezer. The overflowing ashtrays everywhere put me off. He was smoking way too much!

Bob's four younger children grew closer to my kids. On Friday nights, they watched horror movies together, and slept over on my living room floor. I made them pancakes on Saturday mornings and then he would pick up his boys for little league practice. I would then take Kathy home, where she took her job as 'little mother' seriously. She always had laundry and baking planned for Saturdays.

I often saw the DuMouchel children that year without their father. He had gone back to his old job of cutting grass on a golf course. If he was away for extended hours, I would look in on them on my way home from work to make sure they were all right.

One Saturday, five-year-old Jeff showed up in my driveway on his bicycle. "Hey, lady!" (now apparently my nickname) he called, waving as he rolled up.

"Jeff!" I was shocked that he had ridden five and a half miles and crossed a busy highway in what must have been heavy traffic! "What are you doing here Jeffrey? I was just on my way to your house."

He jumped off his bike and walked it into the garage, lowering his head and scuffing at the floor as he explained. "I just wanted to see you and I was afraid you wouldn't come today." I was touched.

Leslie gave Jeff half her cookie, Eddie and Peter put his bicycle in the station wagon and we drove him home.

⸎

The Music Box Theater in St. Petersburg wanted Bob to join their ranks for the coming season. We were invited to an open house where he was asked by James LaRue to sing some of the songs from "Paint Your Wagon."

Then Bob launched into "Secret Love" in his rich, colorful baritone, his eyes focused on mine. The audience applauded wildly, but I didn't hear another sound as he returned to his seat and reached for my hand. That night when he took me home, he held me in his strong arms for a long time. It was a secure, warm feeling and I wanted to stay there forever. When he kissed me, something in his manner made me feel beautiful and cherished. He treated me with such gentleness and respect. I was experiencing something so new, so intense, that when he kissed me again, hungrily, his kisses awoke a sleeping tiger. I felt a desire and passion I simply didn't know I was capable of; something I had never experienced during my marriage to Jim.

We recognized that we were two lonely people and had to be careful with our emotions. After that night, we took great pains to make sure that we always had the children around us. Mike and Steve quickly saw right through this and found it amusing that we spent so much time solving jigsaw puzzles, a pastime, they recognized as a means of keeping our hands off each other.

With childish innocence, Jeff asked me one afternoon, "Hey, lady, are you gonna be my mama?" Suzi picked up his cue from there, talking of nothing else, until there came a time when Bob and I had to explain to them that we were just friends and that neither of us wanted to get married again. They didn't understand, but they let it go, causing us no further embarrassment.

Chapter 7

"High Spirits," a musical version of "Blythe Spirit," was set to open in April of 1969. It is the story of a man who marries for the second time and is haunted by his first wife. This entailed six weeks of rehearsals and a minimum of four weeks of performances in late April and early May at the Showboat Dinner Theater in St. Petersburg.

I had accompanied Bob when he auditioned and was not surprised when he won the male lead. Although I was pleased for him, I knew we would see far less of each other for the next ten weeks. However, the bonds among our children grew, as I continued to wear out the five-and-a-half-mile road between his house and mine.

Mike called me one night, concerned when his Dad had failed to show up at rehearsal, after leaving the house looking despondent. When asked where he was going, he'd told Mike he was going out to get drunk. He was not much of a drinker, having a few beers at the most. Something was definitely wrong.

"Oh, Mike," I said, "has he ever done this before?"

"Not since I've been home. I can't answer about before that, possibly after my mother died."

"No, I really don't think so. He is so devoted to all of you. Something must have happened. Do you think it could be, Jim, my ex? I heard that he and his girlfriend are volunteering as 'gophers' during rehearsals, could they have said something to upset your dad?"

"No," Mike said, "Actually, I've got my own idea about what's bugging him. Maybe you could find a time to talk to him when the kids aren't around. I know he thinks a lot of you and will tell you things he won't tell me."

Since there was nothing I could do, I went to bed, worried. I was still awake when the phone rang an hour later. It was Bob, and the sounds in the background told me he was in a bar.

"Bobby!" I exclaimed, "If you don't come right over, I'm coming after you." I didn't even know where he was, but hopefully he didn't realize that. I dressed quickly, and he arrived fifteen minutes later. He had obviously been nearby.

Two cups of coffee later, we sat on the sofa and he held me in his arms and cried. "I can't do it, I can't go on without June! Please take her place," he implored.

My breath wouldn't come fast enough, and I felt as though I might faint. I was confused and upset but there was only one answer. My heart was enclosed by a fist of ice. I forced myself to speak. "No. I won't, Bob," I said emphatically. "I can't, I'm sorry. Nobody can replace somebody else. Please don't ask that of me."

When he left, I cried bitter tears. Subconsciously I had known we were heading for disaster. I'd left myself wide open. You fool, I thought, why did you let yourself fall in love with him? Oh God, had I actually fallen in love with him? It made no difference, I could not replace June. I felt empty and drained, wakeful all night.

In the cold light of day, I entertained the notion of going back to New Orleans. My grandparents would have room for us and I would happily care for them as they aged. My godfather, Uncle Donald, was managing their affairs, so I called him to see what he thought of the idea. I was crushed by his response.

"No, Lynne. That's not going to happen," he rudely declared, "I've listed their house with a realtor and anticipate that it will sell quickly. The last thing they need, at their ages, is to be accosted by a bunch of screaming kids! You have greatly overestimated your place in this family."

Rebuffed, I then called my Uncle Norman, who handled their insurance. I plead my case, but he didn't encourage me. I then inquired about the smaller Bay St Louis, Mississippi house; asking if I might buy it.

"No, Suga, that's already been sold. We all had an opportunity to bid on it, but nobody wanted the place."

"Why wasn't I asked?" I cried.

"I have to assume Donald offered it to your mother, as he had to the rest of us. When there was no bid from her either, he sold it on the open market." The rejection hurt me more than I realized at the time.

What was left for me? I was so mentally and physically exhausted that I needed a break. For a few days, I refused to answer Bob's calls, finally relenting when my need to see him became overwhelming. We agreed to meet the following Friday night after rehearsal.

"Hey, lady," he imitated Jeff; standing just outside the door, leaning on a tall brick planter. He hadn't knocked. Did he know that I would step outside to look for his car sooner or later? Was he hesitant to knock for fear that he would be rejected again?

"Come in, Bobby," I said flatly, avoiding his eyes. He apologized immediately for what had happened during our last meeting. He tried to impress upon me that asking me to take June's place was not what he had meant. I told him that, nevertheless, I felt that if I married him, I would forever live in her shadow. Not that he had proposed.

We spent a great deal of time talking all around the subject. We discussed the relative merits of keeping his house or mine, his Air Force privileges, schools, finances, and, of course, June. Finally, I couldn't take any more. The whole thing was overwhelming, and I felt tears welling up. I needed air. I excused myself and stepped out into the backyard.

I watched Bob from the darkened patio as he went over to the stereo and put a record on the turntable. If he played "Secret Love," I thought, I would surely cry. Then my heart skipped a beat when I heard the reassuring strains of "Love is Wonderful, the Second Time Around." I pulled myself together and went back inside.

We decided to take Mike and Steve into our confidence; discussing the pros and cons of combining our two families, more like a merger for the sake of both households. But we settled nothing and were no closer to a decision after this meeting either.

On Sunday night, Bob came over to pick up his four youngest, whom I had been watching while he was at rehearsal. That evening, I had been back and forth to their house and answering their calls so often, that I had finally decided to just bring them back home with me. I was being run ragged! I had decided that he needed to hire a nanny or a housekeeper and this was a good time to tell him so.

I asked him to step out onto the porch, away from prying ears, and I flopped down on the daybed. "Bob, I'm sorry," I declared. "I just can't keep doing this, managing two families five miles apart."

"I love you," he said gently. "Will you marry me?"

I looked at him, shocked that the question had been asked and eventually answered softly, "Yes." Tears of relief came as he held me.

"Let's tell the children!" we said in the same breath.

"NOW HEAR THIS," the Sergeant Major bellowed, "ALL YOU KIDS GET OUT ON THIS PORCH ON THE DOUBLE! WE HAVE SOMETHING TO TELL YOU!"

To say they cheered is an understatement.

We chewed over the idea for a few days before we made an appointment at the chapel at MacDill. Bob called for me one afternoon and we drove out to the base admiring all the grand houses along Bayshore Boulevard on peaceful, sparkling Tampa Bay.

The neat, manicured geometry of a military installation with its protocols was familiar to me, having spent time at Ft. Hamilton where my father was stationed in New York. I had lived with Germaine and Bruce and my two brothers in 1954 for only eight months; the longest I had spent with them in my life.

As Bob drove through the base, I noticed all the cars pulling to one side and stopping. Checking my watch, I realized it was time for the American flag to be lowered. We parked just in sight of the flagpole, the Air Force band played "Retreat" over a loudspeaker and we watched as the flag was taken down. It was always impressive.

"Do you miss the Air Force, Bobby?" I asked him.

"Oh, sometimes," he said, "but I've learned to live independently. I spent twenty-two years saying, 'Yes sir'; everything was done for me, even my thinkin', until I was discharged. It's quite a shock for a man in his forties to retire into a world where everyone his age has twenty years' experience in their trade. The only thing I could say was that I had done my job well. Do you want to know what I miss most?"

"What?" I didn't have a clue.

"A hat on my head. Really! Can you imagine wearin' a hat for all those years every time you stepped outdoors, and then goin' without it? It was a natural reflex to reach for a hat whenever I reached for a door."

I laughed, it was so like him to say something trivial to make light of his outstanding career. I was so comfortable with him and he was so good for me.

We saw the Catholic chaplain first. He told us, sympathetically, that he couldn't marry us because I was a divorcee. This came as no surprise. He then sent us down the hall to Reverend John Bonath, the Protestant chaplain. We sat hesitantly in his office and Bob stated our case.

"I have all I can do taking care of my own people," Bonath said, apologetically. "But if you'd like to take instructions and become Methodists, I might be able to marry you."

"Reverend Bonath," Bob insisted, "we are Catholics and will continue to raise our twelve children as Catholics. We can't consider giving up our religion."

"So!" I Interrupted angrily, "You're no better than our priest!" I accused him. "You're turning your back on us, too."

Chaplain Bonath was impressed with our loyalty to our faith and reluctantly relented. His calendar was very full, but he could offer us three available wedding dates. "Day after tomorrow…or May 11th…or July 30th."

When we realized that May 11th was Mother's Day, we decided that was an auspicious day to double our family from six to twelve.

We still had to tell our parents. My folks had gone up to Canada to look at boats. "Dear Dad," I wrote, "I'd love for you to give me away." He had been insulted in 1956 when I asked my granddad, who had reared me, to give me away for my first trip down the aisle.

"To whom and for what?" was his first response, then he wrote, "I presume it's to Bob and for marriage, but you didn't say. I'm sorry that time and expense make it impossible for us to be there." I realized this was an indication that he disapproved of my decision to marry Bob. Dad assumed that he was taking advantage of me. I was hurt, but he had the right to his opinion.

Bob and I couldn't keep our secret for long, as the children were jubilant and told everybody. I wasn't surprised when I received a call from the parish secretary asking me to be at my pastor's office at noon on Monday.

"I'd like to ask you to reconsider your decision to marry again." Monsignor McNulty said, "You will be excommunicated and cause Mr. DuMouchel to be refused the sacraments if he marries a divorcee."

"But divorce action was brought against me, monsignor! Am I supposed to raise my children alone when I have an opportunity to give them another father? A good man who is willing to take on the responsibility of six more…"

"You will find the grace to live alone," he said piously.

"I'm sorry, but I don't agree with you. I believe God will judge us for the positive things we do with our lives. Bob and I are taking the remains of two disasters and creating a new family unit for these twelve children." I was adamant.

My arguments were not new, and I'm sure he didn't call me there to hear what I had to say. On and on he talked about scandal and an unholy atmosphere. He was truly an unworldly man. I wondered if he knew how unholy a home could be when the parents had no respect for each other and seldom shared the same bedroom.

"Promise me that you will think about this second marriage," he said kindly.

"I promise you, I'll think about it," I allowed on my way out.

I was convinced that we have a generous God who put us in this place because we had reached hopelessness in our lives. He meant for us to join forces and make a life for our children; God was giving us a second chance.

Chapter 8

Bob was busy rehearsing "High Spirits" and the time preceding the wedding passed quickly. We counted the days, trying to steal a minute or two alone. Those precious moments when we held each other close, in anticipation of the day we would be husband and wife, were filled with both joy and a sense of regret. Why had I spent so many years shrouded in shame and fear, when life could be so good with the right person?

I spent my evenings sewing frantically to make the girls matching dresses for the wedding. When they were all lined up for their final fitting, they were beautiful; a matched set of my five girls in their blue and white gingham finery.

Whenever I could, I sat in the rehearsal hall watching "High Spirits" take form. The cast sang, "Here comes the bride" when I showed up for the dress rehearsal. All the children followed me into the theater like ducks in a row, in perfect order from Mike down to little Suzi. They watched as Bob played the lead, dancing and singing on the stage. I took all the ribbing the cast could dish out about June haunting Bob and me, and I knew he was over a big hump when he could laugh at their jokes, too.

The Sunday before our wedding, Missy joined the long line of little girls in white dresses and veils receiving their first communion. Bob and I, with eleven of the children, filled two pews in the crowded church. Then, just before the mass began, Jim and Cindy and her twins took seats directly in front of us, as we had planned.

"Hi, Daddy!" Suzi called to Jim. Heads turned, and we saw eyebrows raised among the parishioners around us. After the service, outside in the crowd, Bob was congratulated on his opening night's performance and the circle of onlookers grew as Jim and Cindy approached us. People who knew us fell silent, expecting, no doubt, some sort of confrontation.

"Hello, Jim," Bob said, extending his hand. Jim shook it. "Hi, Bob, nice show last night. See you Wednesday."

There was an audible "aawwhhh" from the crowd as they dispersed, having expected fireworks. We turned our attention to Missy and her sunny, lacy, little classmates, sorted out the children and took our family to my house for Sunday dinner.

That evening, having packed the children off to Betsye's for the night so that I could get some things done, Bob took me into the living room to have what he called a "serious talk."

"Suga," he started, "I need to be straight with you. The thing is, I'm doubtful that I could ever do for you what Jim did." I looked at him quizzically. I simply asked, "What are you talking about?"

"I don't have the stayin' power I used to, sexually. I'm sure Jim could give you multiple orgasms."

"Jim didn't...wait...uh...what exactly is an orgasm?" I asked, honestly.

"You're jokin'?" His eyes were like saucers.

"I don't know what an orgasm is." I was stupidly innocent.

"You really don't know?"

"Really," I admitted honestly. "I've never heard the word before."

He walked away, dumbfounded, leaving me sitting on the sofa. He went to the back of my house, opening and closing doors, letting Sean, our Great Dane, out into the back yard.

"You've really never had an orgasm?" he came back, still incredulous.

"Stop with that!" I insisted. "What's the problem? I was a virgin when I married Jim and have not been with another man."

"Would you like me to show you?" he asked with a grin.

"Please do." He took my hand and led me into the bedroom, shutting the door, even though we were alone. He left at midnight, grinning like a Cheshire cat.

That final week was spent rearranging bedrooms and moving Bob's four youngest children into my house. He was busy in Mango, making our wedding rings out of gold chain, and sweating out good-natured jibes from Mike and Steve, who were setting up their bachelor haven in the Mango house.

We had a few details to clear up before our wedding, and the most significant was how we would handle our finances. Bob claimed that the reason he had no credit cards was because he didn't trust them. I asked delicately if he had good credit and he assured me he did, all over the world, since he had lived so many places while in the service. I didn't understand his reasoning, but why should I care? I had three, one of which was an American Express gold card.

"Just for the sake of autonomy" I said, "I'm putting your name on my accounts."

"OK with me, but not necessary. I won't use them," he said.

Wedding presents came from all over the country, but the nicest was an offer from a courageous couple who agreed to stay with the children while we went on our honeymoon. A friend offered us a long weekend at his house on the Homosassa River, with only a few otters for company. I stocked up on food and washed and ironed everything I could, foregoing the final performance of "High Spirits" and the cast party. Bob phoned after the final curtain to tell me the show had gone well, and that he was not going to the party without me. He would pick me up for mass in the morning to start our wedding day off right.

Chapter 9

Mother's Day 1969 began with sunshine. After church, Bob took his children to the cemetery to put flowers on their mother's grave. Then they were back to collect the rest of us for the drive to MacDill. Jeff bounced up to the door with his usual effervescence, calling, "Hey, lady! We're here!"

The house was filled with friends offering to help; it took many hands to dress the kids. Jo Ann, my maid of honor, brushed all their shiny heads and pinned five little corsages on the girls. Mike pinned on the boys' boutonnieres, all a gift from the Thomases, who grew gardenias. We divided the children into groups, most of whom rode with friends. Mike, our best man, had to drive for us because Bob and I were too nervous. After years of standing in the wings, neither of us expected to experience such stage fright as we did on that day.

Ours was the first car to pull up at the rear of the chapel, thirty minutes later. Bob found the rectory doors locked and went around to the front where two priests were leaving after the last mass. Addressing them, he joked, "All right, I want to thank you fellas for trying to help me get out of this, but would you mind opening the door, so we can get in?"

The chaplain was apologetic as he let me in to the vestibule where I was to wait until the chapel was ready. On a military base, where services of all faiths are held in the same chapel, it is a simple matter to draw drapes and pull cords to rearrange the altar setting for the appropriate denomination. We watched an assistant struggle frantically with a pulley that was supposed to slide the large crucifix aside. The chapel was filling with guests and time was running out. The chaplain finally told the young corpsman to give it up, but he had tugged so strenuously by that time, the massive cross was swaying like a pendulum. They couldn't slow it down, much less stop it. We spent the first few minutes of the beautiful, simple ceremony hypnotized by the swaying crucifix, speaking words in harmony with the rhythm of the huge religious metronome. Francis Goode later commented, "That swinging Jesus was a nice touch, Ducky!"

Eleven of the children were present, along with about thirty of our friends. Bob's mother and father had driven up from Sarasota, but my parents were AWOL. We learned later that Bob's second son, Steve could not get past the MPs at the front gate. He had spent the previous night at a gig with his band, "Mercy". He showed up at MacDill without identification, barefoot and shirtless, wearing a fur-lined vest, many strands of beads, raggedy jeans, a guitar over his shoulder, and hair flowing below his shoulders; the textbook hippie. He was not allowed to enter the installation.

Jeff tugged at the skirt of my little beige lace dress while I was standing in the back ready to walk down the aisle. "Hey, lady," he asked in a loud stage whisper, "is this gonna take long?"

"Hush, Jeffrey," I said. "Go sit with your grandmother in the front pew." He sauntered nonchalantly up the aisle, hands in his pockets and joined Grandpa and Grandma D.

When the priest asked, "Who gives this woman?" Eddie, 9, and Peter, 8, stood up proudly in the front pew and said in bold unison, as they had practiced, "We do!" Actors from two theaters, including the entire cast from "High Spirits" tittered and applauded.

After the ceremony, as Bob and I turned to leave the altar, Jeff hopped in between us and walked out holding each of our hands. When we got to the vestibule, he raised his little arms up to me and said, "Hey, Mama!" His broad, happy face beamed up at me, and I was overwhelmed with joy. I leaned over and hugged my new little boy.

We then crossed the base to the NCO Club for a champagne toast for the adults and punch for the kids. Alice Smith, a staff photographer for the Brandon News, had offered to take a picture of our new family as her wedding gift. "Of course, Alice, what a lovely idea, thank you!" I said, with the codicil that she not spread us all over the paper where she was employed. Of course, we returned home to find ourselves on the front page.

Pat, Bob, Suga, Mike, and Dan
Eddie, Jane, Kathy, and Peter
Missy, Jeff, Suzi, and Leslie

Sean had not been consulted about this marriage and was not exactly in favor; something we had not considered. I had found him in Stone Mountain, Georgia the year we moved to Atlanta. Sean was truly a Great Dane. At the age of five he stood over three and a half feet high on all fours, weighed in at 175 pounds, and his blue-black coat would allow him to disappear in the dark had it not been for his bright yellow eyes. And what a watch dog! No matter what was going on, he watched, that's all, just watched. He would raise his eyelids enough to let the light in, and watch. But his size alone made us feel safe. If he ever stood on his hind legs, he'd be taller than an average man, and only a determined, courageous interloper would try to push past him. He would probably only have his face licked, but the potential intruder wouldn't know that.

Delivery men had to be escorted past him. One truck driver laid on his horn when Sean was sunning himself on the front lawn. The timid driver was afraid to get out of his cab. His multitude of cartons were more than I would have been able to carry, so I called out, "He won't bite," trying to allay his fears, but not even a bribe could coerce him to trust me.

"I promise you the dog won't bite!" I shouted, again.

"Yeah, lady," he replied, "You know that, and I know that, but does he know that?"

With us, Sean was as comfortable as an old shoe. He allowed the children to flop all over him when they sprawled on the floor to watch TV. If he felt the need for a nap, he covered his ear with one paw and shut his eyes. If he truly couldn't stand the program the kids were watching, he squirmed until they rolled aside, and gingerly rising to his feet, would move into another room.

When he was young, Sean was an excellent babysitter on the beach, never losing sight of the children. By some mysterious means, he knew how many he was responsible for at any given time and was selfish with his wards. No other child, and certainly no adult, could come near them unless he got the word from me. Also, he wouldn't allow a child to swim in water over his own belly. That was acceptable when the kids were little, but as they got bigger, their desire to swim grew, and the situation became touchy. He gave us no trouble when he was chained to a stake, so we could enjoy deeper water without being 'rescued'.

We were unprepared for the way his protectiveness manifested itself when Bob and I returned from our honeymoon. On the first night back in my old bedroom, Sean was displeased that a new man, no matter how well loved, was getting into bed with me. He bared his teeth, rested his muzzle inches from Bob's head on his pillow and with eyes flashing, let out a rumbling, intimidating growl from deep in his throat, "Grrrrrrrr!"

"Honey," Bob whispered, "call off your dog."

"I don't think he'll bother you." I said quietly, consoling him.

"Well I don't want to find out! He growls dangerously," he whispered.

"I think it's kind of dear that he protects me so much. Go to sleep, Bobby, and don't worry about him." Bob kept his hands to himself and tried to ignore his growling companion's muzzle, less than ten inches away.

Days later, my guard dog still kept his vigil, rumbling deep in his throat if Bob so much as stirred or raised his hand. Pretty soon my groom's patience ran out and this time when he asked me to call off the dog, I tried but failed. Sean was determined to guard me from this intruder. By the second week, my poor husband was exasperated, and, mustering his courage and strength, he dragged Sean by his spiked collar all the way to the garage. He then tiptoed back, smug and triumphant, into the bedroom and climbed into bed. A split second later, we heard SLAM! and Sean trotted proudly back through the house, having flattened the kitchen door.

After a few months, Sean adjusted to sharing my affection with his new master. Bob had performed before many audiences in the past and this was just another. It was no longer necessary to bolt the bedroom door.

Chapter 10

We settled into a comfortable family routine over the next few months. I cooked a lot of pasta with meat sauce, a lot of burgers on the grill, and Bob prepared gargantuan meals in his giant pressure cooker.

While we had our sights on finding a larger place we could afford, Bob concentrated on working out a system for the children to pitch in with the house and yard work. Each big kid was assigned a little kid and they worked together. The Mouton children were the principal grumblers since they had enjoyed maids through the years, but the DuMouchels just seemed grateful to have a woman in the house.

We watched as a romance developed between Diana Fernandez and Michael. My dear friend, Diana, ten years my junior, with whom I had shared the stage, was to become my daughter-in-law. Before long, we were up to our earrings in wedding plans. Jeff was fitted with a formal morning suit for his role as ring bearer and Suzi was chosen as flower girl. I made her a darling yellow dress to match the bridesmaids. She was a picture, carrying a basket of daisies and posing confidently with her new little brother for pictures.

Missy had her flower girl debut when her godmother, Betty Ann Bordes, married in New Orleans the previous year. Betty had been my flower girl in 1956 and we considered this the continuation of a tradition. I had been Betty's mother's (Aunt Cyril) flower girl and we anticipated Betty's child would be Missy's, but fate had other plans.

Missy's little escort for Betty's wedding, a timid three-year-old, plopped himself squarely on the floor after he took only two steps. Missy was not deterred; she was going to have her walk down the aisle! She grabbed him by one arm and literally dragged him on his rear the rest of the way to the altar, to the delight of everyone in the church.

After months of planning, Jo Ann Shearn's wedding came off without a hitch on a sunny Saturday in June. No thanks to me.

I had completed her gown, but just back from my own honeymoon, I fell behind on her bridesmaids' dresses. Jo Ann had chosen the style, provided the material, and I had whipped up their gowns before Bob and I got married, including buttonholes. But in my haste, I had failed to cover the buttons. This, I learned from my grandmother when I was very young, is the sign of a first class, custom-made garment. I had, in turn, taught my daughters to make covered buttons and they practiced until they were proficient.

When the wedding day arrived, two shiny black limousines idled in front of our house as four beautifully made-up and coiffed young ladies stood in their petticoats in my sewing room. The girls balanced from one unfamiliar high heel to the other, bare backs exposed because their dresses gaped open forlornly awaiting their covered buttons.

Now, covering a button to match a garment is simply a matter of sandwiching a small circle of matching fabric between two round metal caps and snapping them together, leaving a bit of the cloth underneath, in the center, for attaching to the garment. Kathy, 10, Jane, 9, Leslie, 8, and Missy, 7, worked frantically to cover the bridesmaids' sixty buttons! Suzi, 6, then handed each to me. One at a time I quickly sewed them onto the four lovely pink dresses, buttoned each one, and ushered the girls out the front door and into the limos. With all accounted for, the drivers then sped to the wedding chapel. My little girls, laughing, giggling and exhausted, collapsed on the carpet.

Bob hustled me into our car and on to the church. I dashed to the bride's room where Jo Ann was dressing, zipped her up, secured her veil on her head and led her to her father in the doorway of the chapel. She and her dad started down the aisle, and Bob's wonderful baritone voice rang out as he sang "The Lord's Prayer" from the choir loft. The show must go on, in the great tradition of the theater.

Now, reader, I'll give away my secret. You may have noticed I said, "zipped her up"? A bridal gown is usually voluminous and delicate, yet cumbersome. For me to make a bride stand anxiously through several fittings while I slipped thirty-six tiny loops over thirty-six satin-covered buttons from her neck to her butt, would have been tortuous. A clever, experienced dressmaker sews the three-dozen satin-covered buttons encased in the loops beforehand, on top of the fold that will conceal the zipper! Voila!

Chapter 11

Diana was visiting her grandmother, so Mike and Steve came over in a driving rain for Sunday dinner and brought a whole ham. While it was being glazed and heated, and the chickens roasted with veggies, the younger kids passed the rainy afternoon playing games in our big double garage. Bob and the two big boys were smoking up the house, all four of us reading the Tampa Tribune, exchanging the funnies, when Jeffrey came in from the garage. He stood politely, fidgeting a bit in front of his father until Bob put down the paper and looked squarely at the boy.

"Uh...Honcho?" Jeffrey began quietly.

"Yes, Jeff," Bob feigned impatience.

"Uh, Honcho, how...uh hot..., uh, how hot does a...um, license plate have to get before it uh...melts?"

"I can't be sure, but I would guess about 1500 degrees. Why do you want to know that?" he spoke loudly and firmly, his eyes opened wide. He was justifiably alarmed.

"Well, uh..., you know that car...that, er, station wagon, the red one ...uh...in the garage?"

"Yes. What about it?" Bob dropped the paper on the floor and stood up slowly.

"Well, uh...Honcho, you see that license plate, the one...um, on that car, ...it, ...uh...melted."

Mike, Steve, and I silently put down our papers and joined Bob as he followed Jeff out to the garage. The rest of the children were standing at the rear of the car, staring at the license plate. Not one said a word, looking furtively at the car, then up at us.

"Move over," Bob ordered, while we crowded behind the car and the children shuffled out of our way. The plate was melted, no question about it. Numbers drooped in saggy painted waves, and the shape of the metal was irregular, dipping down an inch in places.

"What did you guys do?" Bob addressed the strangely quiet children, his severe voice frightening them. All ten denied any wrongdoing. We asked them questions, but no answers were provided.

"Did you do this, Jeffrey?" Bob touched the license plate, it was cool to the touch.

"No, sir, I was just the one who saw it first," he said proudly.

There were no chemicals in the garage, no tools of destruction, no welding torch, and not one of those ten kids would own up to melting it. For days we tried but could glean no answers from them. We assumed they had made some sort of a pact to keep the secret, because no matter what we threatened or offered as a reward, they would not tell.

I took the horribly deformed plate to the tag office in Plant City where they issued new ones.

"What happened to this tag?" a pleasant clerk asked.

"I don't know," I had to admit, feeling like a fool.

"Did the car catch fire?" she asked.

"No, nothing like that. My children did something to it," I said, embarrassed.

"Do you mind talking with my supervisor, Mr. Flannery?" queried the clerk.

Is it a crime to destroy a license plate, I wondered? Am I in trouble?

"I'm willing to pay for a new one," I added.

"That won't be necessary, please wait, ma'am. He may want to ask a few questions." In fact, he asked the same question we all had, but there was no answer. He laughed a bit, and simply asked if they could keep the ruined plate to display on their wall. It is probably still there. I wish I had kept it.

Jo Ann's mother had entered her daughter's wedding dress in the fashion competition at the state fair and it won first place. The gown would be celebrated at the fashion exhibit tent in a mock wedding. It was to be worn by the bride herself, who would parade down the ramp on the final and busiest day of the fair. This was a major event, attended by hundreds of people and photographers from several newspapers.

Jo Ann called me, in tears. Would I wear the dress for her? She was thrilled by the recognition, as was I, but she was over-whelmed with morning sickness and could not risk going out in public that day, or any day. She was sure she was going to die.

The only problem with my standing in for the bride was, Jo Ann was a size 20, while I was slightly under a 10. To distract from her girth, I had designed the sleeves to catch the eye. Jo Ann had beautiful hands, so I finished off the long sleeves with a cascade of Alençon lace at her wrists. The simple front of the gown was basically smooth satin, but the back was my specialty. In a wedding, the congregation primarily sees the back when a bride stands at the altar, and that's where I shone. I began with a series of lined scallops at the waist, overlapping each layer, graduating to larger-over-larger scallops down the back, ending in huge three-foot wide scallops at the end of the long train. The image was that of beautiful white scales, reminiscent of a mer-maid! I had considered it a masterpiece, my pièce de résistance. I assured her everything would be fine and agreed to wear the gown for her. With no time for alterations, I wore it as it was, calculating the weight of the back would hold the front flush against my body as I walked.

My pretend groom was a skinny teenager, not old enough to shave, wearing white tie and tails many sizes too big for him. I walked proudly on his arm like a good actress. To my surprise, all twelve of the children and Bob sat together at the foot of the long ramp cheering me on, yelling out "Yeah, Mom!" and "Way to go, Mom!" Jeffrey stood up on a chair so that everyone could see and hear him shout triumphantly, "That's my Mama!"

Chapter 12

"Seventeen-room house completely furnished.
Low down payment.
Immediate occupancy
Call A. Rittman at XXX-XXXX."

The ad caught my eye. We needed more space! How many of those rooms were bedrooms, I wondered? I called the number on Sunday afternoon, and learned that the property was in Port Tampa. Bob was at work and the kids were at Betsye's house for a cookout. So, I recruited Michael and Diana to go with me to check the place out.

The house was on Mascotte Street, just one mile from where Bob was dockmaster at Imperial Yacht Basin, and only two miles from MacDill AFB where we had medical and commissary privileges! One corner boasted a bronze historical marker telling of Teddy Roosevelt's exploits in the Spanish American War, landing his Rough Riders on the sailing ship, "Mascotte", at this spot. While the location was ideal, and the area was still loaded with charm, that part of town had gone steadily downhill.

We liked the house from the outside. It was three stories high, reminiscent of many grand old houses in New Orleans. I had the feeling it had been loved and the salesman confirmed my theory. He pointed out the newly painted, wide screened porch running the length of the house. Four chairs, on the otherwise dilapidated old porch, were painted bright blue. A touch of lipstick on the 'old girl', I suspected, to make the old homestead more presentable.

"Mr. Hicks painted the porch himself before he put it on the market," the agent explained. "Since he wasn't able to paint the entire house, he hoped it would help the buyer see the potential. Cecil Hicks was born in this house eighty-some years ago. He played in that giant oak out front, and do you see that magnolia?" He gestured toward a tall blossoming tree alongside what must have been a bedroom window in the rear. "When Cecil was seven years old, he planted that magnolia for his mother on Mother's Day. We've been friends for more than thirty years, and when he finally moved out, he asked me to sell his home to a family with children who could grow up and be happy here; someone who would take care of the house and love it. It's been divided into three apartments for rentals, but that can easily be remedied." I brushed a beaded cobweb from a window and peered through at the colorless interior.

"We would like to look around inside, please, Mr. Rittman," Michael said.

Mike and Diana helped me pace off rooms. The house needed repair, but Bob was a magician with tools. Every room was basically square, but a few walls could be removed, and the space repurposed to fit our needs. What remained of the furniture was 'early attic', and no less than five coats of paint adorned every wooden surface. The greatest shame of all was a magnificently carved stair rail and banister, obviously from a grand era, but it had been painted and painted and painted until the carving lost its shape in puddles of white enamel. Lots of elbow grease would be needed, but we could strip the entire stairway and return it to its original beauty.

Faded, threadbare linoleum covered most of the flooring and termite damage had been repaired by an amateur who meant well but was not up to the task. The price was certainly right and there was a vacant lot included that would make a terrific football field for our homegrown team.

Being from New Orleans, I was naturally attracted by the sprawling verandas and the magnolia tree. Also, the back yard boasted two pecan trees larger than any I had ever seen, and there was a storage shed just a few steps from the back door. I instinctively knew Bob would love it.

The next day I packed hot dogs, buns and condiments, sodas and a watermelon, plus of course, all the children. After work, Bob met us at the property so that we could look it over together. Mr. Rittman walked Bob through, then left us to talk, saying he'd come back later to lock up. Our kids ran through the house, swarming like roaches, whooping and hollering, enjoying the echoes and vibrations when they clomped up and down the uncarpeted stairs. The boys found a tiny porch upstairs that extended almost into the branches of the giant oak in front. Most of the bedrooms had windows that opened right onto the roof of the porches, so they planned secret escapes by way of the roof and the trees.

Afterwards, we cooked out in a quaint little triangular park a block from the house, and after they had eaten and worn themselves out, we had a chance to talk about what we had seen. Our conversation was suddenly interrupted by a train passing not ten feet away. In our excitement, we had failed to notice tracks running alongside the park and we watched the switchmen guide the noisy old cars into a railroad yard in the next block.

"What do you think about the train being so close, Bobby?" I asked, hoping it wouldn't discourage him.

"What train?" he replied.

We signed papers the next day. Mr. Hicks agreed to hold the $6,500 mortgage, payable in monthly installments. An Allstate agent came out and wrote a policy. The most he would insure the old beauty for was $10,000, which sounded fair.

Rather than wait a few weeks to move properly, in June of 1969, I began making trips in my station wagon to clean and prepare the house; each day I brought boxes of books or linens, carload by carload, transferring our world. On one trip, with two of the boys to tote boxes, I was greeted by a darling white-haired lady in her eighties. She told me she had known the Hicks family all her life. She had been most unhappy over the last few years when transient families had been allowed to rent parts of the house.

"My dear," she confided, "the whole neighborhood is happy the Hicks house is sold. The last tenant just overran the street with children!"

I gulped. Danny and Eddie looked slyly over at me, challenging me with their eyes to tell her the truth about our family.

"Mrs. Robinson," I asked hesitantly, "how many children did the last people have?"

"Seven!" she snorted, "Seven noisy, grimy boys."

I would eventually learn to let people adjust to us slowly, but those were the early days and I plowed right ahead.

"We also have seven sons, Mrs. Robinson, and five daughters." She looked aghast. I decided it wasn't necessary to explain that Mike and Steve didn't live with us, ten are just as formidable as a dozen. Maybe I could see to it that they weren't too grimy, but I'd have to depend on the trains to drown out the daily noise.

I wish I could say things went smoothly, but we encountered a major problem when I submitted a large catalog order to Sears that I had compiled over the first two months in the house.

"Sorry, Mrs. DuMouchel," a clerk phoned to say, "we can't honor this purchase. Sgt. DuMouchel has a long record of unpaid balances in Alaska, Newfoundland and Germany." I was stunned.

I didn't know if it was because he had been protected by the service all his adult life, or if he had to lie about money to keep it away from June. I detected a deadly pattern, and a lie too big to overlook! I had been managing our accounts with his blessing and I already knew I couldn't trust him to tell me the truth about what he spent. He had even written a check for two hundred dollars to two young men we hired to paint the interior of my Brandon house, but only wrote "twenty dollars" in the check register. That was his convoluted way of keeping the balance intact! More than once he overspent to the point where I had trouble paying the utilities. He was always contrite and promised to do better. I wanted to trust him, so I inquired gently, "Bobby," I asked calmly, "what do you think we can do about this problem?" I winced, and he asked, "Headache?"

"No thanks I've already got one," I said flatly, "And it's a whopper!"

"I'm sorry, Suga, I have never handled money well," he confessed.

"How did you get by, Bobby?? You had to pay bills, didn't you?" He looked down at the floor, just the way Jeff so often did when he was ashamed.

"Please don't hang your head. This is serious, I want you to tell me what I'm supposed to do," I persisted. He avoided looking at me while he offered his solution.

"I want you to take the checkbook and the credit cards away from me and just give me cigarette money. This is worse than you know. I had a house and a car repossessed in Nebraska. My dad pulled us out of trouble more times than I can remember."

I tore up my list for Sears, deciding to get by with what we had.

My Brandon house rented quickly, so it had to be emptied sooner than we had anticipated. A bank president from Georgia was ready to relocate his family and he gave us a deposit plus the first and last month's rent. The furniture from both our houses was transferred to Port Tampa and literally stacked against the walls until we could weed it out. Keeping the best from all three houses for our new funny farm, Mike and Steve then took what they needed to occupy the Mango house, and the rest was given away. One kitchen in the rear was turned into a laundry for our four daily loads of wash. There was enough room for the freezer, ironing board and a large table for folding clothes. We sold the stove from the second-floor kitchen but retained the rest as a 'day-room' for the kids; in military parlance, that means a "hang out room". The refrigerator and table would be useful. Cabinets and counters were ideal for the overflow of puzzles and hobbies, and in the summer the children had breakfast up there, minimizing the work in my main kitchen below.

I claimed a tiny room downstairs for my sewing machine, two chests of fabric and patterns.

Next came the assignment of bedrooms, no small chore, trying to divide twelve people into the luxury of seven bedrooms. It had been simple in Brandon, bunks in the boys' room, bunks in the girls' room, stacked to the ceiling.

The older boys at home were Peter, 11, Eddie and Pat, both 12, and Danny, nearly 15. They didn't want little Jeffrey hanging out with them. We told all five to get together and come up with a plan. When they couldn't reach any satisfactory solution, Bob resolved it one night at dinner when he announced that the three boys who happened to be sitting on one side of the table would share a room and the two across from them would get the bedroom next to it. They would share a bath and their ages had nothing to do with the arrangement. Amen.

The girls also had their difficulties. Missy and Suzi were considered the "little girls" and would share a room; Jane and Kathy were "big" and Leslie Anne, at 8, was a "neither-nor" by their standards.

There were definite advantages to having the two youngest girls together. Their bedtime was earlier and their toys and tastes in clothes were the same.

Since the big girls now shared their crushes and secrets, they didn't want Leslie in their room. I simply put another single bed in their large room and told Leslie she was moving.

"But Mom, she'll read our diaries!" Jane and Kathy objected, whining.

My solution, I bought Leslie a little diary and showed her how to use it. The caveat, which she grasped immediately, was if she touched the big girls' diaries, they could read hers. So be it.

My roommate seemed satisfied to have me share his bedroom and I was only too happy to do so. We chose a large corner room on the first floor for our master suite. Windows on two sides opened onto the screened porch, away from foot traffic, so when the children went upstairs at night to watch TV, we had all the privacy we wanted.

As you can imagine, managing a household the size of ours required organization and discipline. Our duty roster was a gem, designed, of course, by Master Sergeant Honcho. Revolving each month, it had nine chores, assigned to nine kids, plus a tenth which was the 'acting sergeant.' His/her job was to see that all the others did their jobs, or else he/she had to do it! It was a daily challenge to keep order and get things done, which fell to me, but the kids were remarkably helpful. It was a big game to them. I recall seeing six-year-old Acting Master Sergeant Suzi pointing a finger at her big brother. "Danny," she called in her biggest voice, "you get out there and cut that grass!" And he did.

To maintain maximum control with minimum confusion early on, Bob and I worked out a plan. Danny, Pat, Eddie, Peter and Kathy were considered big kids. Jane, Leslie, Jeffrey, Missy, and Suzi were little kids. We assigned to each big kid a little kid, with instructions to share their laundry day, (they all learned to do their wash), and to teach the little kid everything he or she knew. They were also responsible for "their kid" on family outings. Their job was to bring that little kid home. "Don't ever come home without him!" read a sign on the door.

Once we moved to Port Tampa, they all used the same last name and we did not use the term "step" at all. They had no problem calling me mom and Bob, dad or Honcho, and they embraced the idea of new brothers and sisters. This went smoothly from day one. Bob painted a big sign that he hung with pride over the door onto the porch. It stated in elegant Edwardian script:

"DuMouchel's Domicile"

We had not anticipated the problem that arose in the new school, where we registered all the kids as "DuMouchel". Our thought was simply to enforce a sense of togetherness and unity, and legality be damned. They considered us both to be authentic parents, and they couldn't be identified by their looks, because in recent summer days, the sun had bleached all their young heads blonde, and many had blue eyes.

Peter and Kathy's sixth-grade teacher, Linda Swain, singled them out after they had filled out class information cards. She called them up in front of the class.

"One of you is not telling the truth on your card," she said, expecting to expose some sort of trickery. "It is physically impossible for a brother and sister in the same family to be the same age with one of you born in June and the other in December. Now, which one of you has written down the wrong birth year?" The two kids looked squarely at the teacher, then furtively at each other. Kathy, being somewhat timid, nervously twisted a tissue in her hands as big tears formed in her eyes and spilled down her cheeks. No one in the class made a sound.

"Well?" Ms. Swain said. Peter knew he had to speak up, as the teacher was growing impatient. She tapped her foot and frowned at them.

"We're both telling the truth!" he said finally. "One of us is a stepchild, but we forget which one!"

"Oh," said the teacher. "Then one of you is real and the other one is a stepchild. Which is which?"

Kathy spoke softly, just loud enough so the class could hear her response. "We're both real, Ms. Swain." She and Peter nodded.

The class erupted in spontaneous giggles, breaking the tension. Realizing she had misspoken, Ms. Swain apologized, and the matter was put to rest. Neither Peter nor Kathy mentioned this to us when they got home from school that afternoon. Later in the evening, Ms. Swain called the house, and after she recounted the incident, sincerely apologized. Blended families were a rarity in those days. "Mrs. DuMouchel," she said humbly, "I'm so sorry! Obviously, they both feel truly loved, and I just wasn't thinking…"

I interrupted, "Actually, Ms. Swain, thank you for calling. We don't allow them to talk back to grown-ups, but in this case, Peter is absolutely correct. They're technically both 'stepchildren', though we refuse to use that term. My husband told the children that the only steps we'll ever have in our house are the ones that lead up to the front door. We have a combined family with three sets of kids born in the same years. Ours is like the Brady Bunch times two!"

Chapter 13

There came a day, many months and many dollars later, when bright, happy wallpaper and fresh paint greeted us everywhere. On the first floor, brick patterned vinyl flooring, new kitchen cabinets, and bookcases reaching to the nine-foot ceilings were only a few of our accomplishments. Ancient rusty plumbing had been replaced and a beautiful authentic brick fireplace was exposed when an interior wall came down.

The house was built before indoor plumbing, so when water was added to the interior, the pipes matriculated on the outside. The children found those pipes both fascinating and an excellent means of escape when they couldn't get out to the upper porches and into trees like monkeys. "Please, please, children," I begged, "use the doors like real people!"

We worked together, handing out age appropriate jobs to the kids, all of whom were proud of what they learned and contributed to the restoration. Some scrubbed, some sawed or sewed, a few painted, everyone swept, and before long it began to feel warm and inviting. I had so much fabric in my stash, it was easy to brighten the rooms with colorful curtains and quilts. Our family brought the old house and the neighborhood back to life.

The first big occasion after we were settled was July 20,1969; both Jane and Honcho celebrated birthdays and that night we watched our small television screen (it was about the size of a 21-inch computer monitor) as Neil Armstrong walked on the moon!

We adapted musical performances from the vast number of 78 rpm records we had of Broadway shows. Each of the children chose a role for every production and I shared with the kids all I had learned about dance when I worked for Arthur Murray. Bob's boys had beautiful voices, Eddie and Peter, not so much.

Our previously child-adverse neighbor, Mrs. Robinson, grew to love the young ones, often handing out homemade cookies. She gave Jeff little paid jobs when she needed him. Sometimes he would stay with her while her daughter was out. "Lady sitting," he called it. On many occasions, she would hire him to "chicken sit" when she was away herself. He became quite good at feeding her chickens and collecting eggs, most of which she donated to us.

As our first Christmas approached, we planned to make it special. Bob received an early bonus and we went shopping for ten bicycles, asking each merchant if we might qualify for a quantity discount. The shopkeepers all refused, suspicious that we would, in turn, resell them for a profit. Discouraged, we armed ourselves with our wedding picture which showed all the kids. Finally, an amused and generous store manager agreed, but declined to assemble the bikes. Bob considered this a plus, because transporting ten assembled bicycles presented another problem. We accepted ten boxes, which were squirreled from my station wagon into a storeroom at the marina where Bob could assemble them in his free time.

A phone call from the Tampa Tribune presented a new dilemma. Our bicycle store manager had blown our secret! The reporter wanted to photograph all ten kids receiving their bikes for the front page of the Christmas edition! We had to refuse; our kids were not to see the gift until after church on Christmas

Day. He compromised, and we agreed he could come a few days ahead to gather pictures of the family and write the story of our merger, with no mention of the bikes.

That settled, I realized that I was not ready to be photographed. My hair hadn't been done since our wedding. I panicked, calling every beauty salon in Port Tampa, all of which were booked solid from December 20th through Christmas. I bemoaned my failure while Bobby and I shared our lunch at the marina.

"Not to worry, my princess, old Bobby DuMouchel will get you an appointment. Give me the number of the salon you want." I cautiously handed him the phone number. He dialed.

"As if they're going to let you make an appointment for me!" I protested. He held up his hand when someone answered.

"Madame!" Bobby said with a perfect French accent. "My name is Monsieur DuMouchel, and I'm in this country on business, but my wife, chu! The way she look, I can take her no place!! Can you fix her?" Silence.

"Ah ha, oui, madame, merci beaucoup! And, please, you need to know she speaks no English so good as me. What time? Oui, oui, merci, madame." He hung up, raising his eyebrows at me.

"You weren't talking to anybody, Bobby," I insisted.

"One o'clock, Madame DuMouchel, and you'd better be there," he replied with a grin.

"No way, Bobby, I'm not going to walk into that place without an appointment. I called them an hour ago and they had no time for me." I was still doubtful.

"Get your ass in gear, madame, you have an appointment in less than one hour. Now get!" He turned me around and literally pushed me to the door.

Reluctantly, I drove the mile home, washed my face and headed to the shop, fully expecting to be turned away. I parked and went in, timidly. A large, buxom woman in a black smock, looking up at the clock, came right to me. "**Are you Madame DuMouchel?**" she asked loudly.

I nodded, as she took my purse and led me, like a child, to her station. I thought she was going to pick me up and put me in the chair, but she only helped me climb up, then swished a large cape over me, tying it in the back. Then she shouted, as we tend to do when speaking to someone who doesn't understand our language, "**What are we going to do for you, madame?**"

Since I "don't speak good English," I raised two fingers and made a gesture like scissors opening and closing.

"**Ah hah! We cut!**" She then flopped the chair back down until my head was in the shampoo bowl. After a double shampoo and rinse I was flipped up to a sitting position and hair began cascading to the floor as she cut.

"Who do you think she is?" the girl in the next station asked with raised eyebrows, reflected in the mirror.

"I don't have any idea," my operator answered, "but her husband is an ambassador or something."

"Where from?" the other girl asked.

"Damned if I know, but he's somebody important!" she replied as I stared into the mirror, determined to keep my mouth shut, thinking smugly, an ambassador? No, a damned good actor!

She shaped my hair nicely, set it in rollers, then put me under a dryer. I could barely hear, but the other operators came to stare straight at me and ask more questions. My operator then put two magazines in my lap, and instead of letting me look at them, she flipped pages and pointed forcibly to the pictures. Fortunately, she didn't feel the need to read it to me. Obviously, I not only didn't speak good English, but I was a nincompoop in her eyes! By the time my hair dried, I had heard speculation of every kind from other operators who, stooping over to look curiously at me under the dryer, suggested all manner of things, to include my being the wife of a king. All this buzzing around while I maintained a straight face with difficulty.

By the end of the hour, my hair had been combed out in a becoming style. She held up a mirror to show me the back, and I was genuinely pleased. Now I had to figure out a way to mime payment since I had no clue as to what they charged. I dumped the entire contents of my purse onto the counter with a questioning expression. I shrugged my shoulders and held out my hands in supplication. My stylist gingerly pulled a few loose bills from the contents and shook each one in front of me. I then grabbed another bill and put it in her pocket for a tip. Amazingly, she then carefully returned everything to my purse.

"Would you like another appointment?" she shouted at me. I just maintained my blank look. She rolled her hands like a cheerleader, saying, **"Again**?" I nodded my head to indicate "yes." Then she said, looking in her book, holding up two fingers **"Next week? Two o'clock**?" to which I bobbed my head enthusiastically, saying, "Deux!"

"Yes, yes!" she bellowed, **"Next week, deux o'clock! You come back deux o'clock!"** I smiled broadly in agreement as I backed out the door.

When I got in my car, I was ready to explode, having stayed in character all that time. I pulled over when I got out of sight and laughed myself silly. I called a few days later, claiming to be Madame DuMouchel's secretary and cancelled the appointment. I had neither the time nor the money to spend in beauty parlors.

Later that afternoon the Tampa Tribune reporter showed up with a photographer and posed the children around the Christmas tree, each holding small wrapped gifts. Not one of the kids said a word about the humble stack of presents, nor did they suspect we had something better for them.

The Christmas edition had a full page spread about us, entitled, "One + One = Twelve!" They had also taken pictures outside when we told them what had happened the first time we rang the dinner bell. Unknown to us, another large family in our new neighborhood also summoned their children with a big bell and the first time Bob rang ours, twenty children raced down the sidewalk and up onto our porch! We eventually worked things out with the other family, who, fortunately, had a triangle they could ring instead of a bell to summon their flock, a distinctly different sound.

The Tribune photographer wanted a picture of that, too, wanting to see this daily event for himself. The poor man was nearly run over, standing right in the path of ten stampeding DuMouchels.

After mass on Christmas Day, I drove the kids to the marina to wish Honcho a Merry Christmas. The pandemonium when they walked into that building, seeing ten beautiful new bicycles lined up, was amazing! The four big boys gravitated to the larger bikes, but not before helping Suzi, Missy, Jeffrey and Leslie find theirs. Jane and Kathy were on their own. When they calmed down, they hugged and kissed and thanked us over and over. I had them line up outside for a picture, then ride the mile to our house, in single file with me creeping alongside in the car.

That night, when the kids were all tucked in upstairs, Bobby and I opened a bottle of champagne and congratulated ourselves on a secret well kept. I had made him a maroon velvet caftan which he loved, and he presented me with a solid gold thimble. Impractical, because gold is too soft, but I never let on.

Christmas 1969

People often gawked at our big family, but we held our heads up proudly. It was amazing how often we were asked "Why did you have so many children?" I developed an elaborate answer: "You really want to know? Well, four children are too much for anyone, you simply can't work more in a day than you do with four small children. Hopefully, by the time the fourth one comes along, you have at least one four-year old, so you have one who can answer the phone. Also, by that time, three of the four are walking. So, a fifth just blends in, as does the sixth. It makes no appreciable difference. Then when you add the second six, you just cook in a bigger pot, add more water to the soup, and you assign a list of small jobs they each can handle. Then you're home free and you can let your fingernails grow." I'd smile sweetly into their blank faces. They appeared to be satisfied but didn't realize their question remained unanswered. My routine worked so well I taught it to Bobby and before long the older kids developed their own versions.

Bob had a lot of free time each day when the boaters had come and gone, and it was not as busy on the weekdays, so he amused himself by fishing. He fashioned a stout broomstick into a fishing pole, a necessity, because he was going to fish for snook, which are strong fierce fighters. They normally hide under shadowy docks, and he had lots of those to choose from. Never discouraged, he worked at it diligently for weeks until the day he called and asked, "Suga, do you have a minute to come here and pick up dinner?" I drove down immediately and picked up the fattest, biggest snook I had ever seen.

That afternoon, before he cleaned it, he wanted to weigh his trophy. "How can you weigh this thing?" I asked. I could hardly hold it once it was unwrapped. He tried getting on a scale himself holding his fish, cold from its nap in the refrigerator. That didn't work.

"Get the kids," he suggested. He then directed Jeff, Leslie, Missy and Suzi to lie down next to each other on the floor alongside the fish, while the bigger kids looked on, perplexed. They assumed he was going to take a crazy picture. He then excused Jeff, Leslie and Suzi. Missy turned out to be the same length as the fish. I was just watching this, wondering what conclusion he could draw, until he said, "Suga, go weigh Missy, please."

We called it a twenty-one-pound snook! No one ever argued with Honcho's measuring methods, and when they laughed and spoke of it, years later, they always called that snook, "Missy's fish."

We made a fine court-bouillon that evening, a very special seafood delight. That is a French delicacy, pronounced "coor-boo-yon". It means, basically, 'food for a king' (or the court). Everyone wanted to help.

I placed one entire fileted side of the fish, coated with butter, skin side down, in a very large Pyrex baking dish. I made a dressing of onions, celery, peppers, garlic, diced cooked shrimp and breadcrumbs, and packed it on tightly, about an inch thick. I then moistened it with water left from boiling the shrimp, covered the dressing with the other filet, buttered skin side up, and covered it with a light tomato-based, seasoned sauce. It was then baked under foil in a 325-degree oven. Fit for a king!! Not a crumb was left over, and it was worthy of our culinary hall of fame, along with Honcho's corned beef and cabbage. Somehow, in comparison, cooking a turkey or a pork roast was just not memorable. But I couldn't take all the credit. After all, Bob caught, cleaned, scaled and fileted the fish, Missy happened to be the same size, and the two big girls, Jane and Kathy, chopped garlic, red and green bell pepper, onions and celery. Suzi, standing on a chair, had washed and dried the vegetables. Leslie stirred the mix. Eddie opened and diluted three cans of tomato paste, which I seasoned with lemon pepper. Jeffrey stood on a chair and stirred the sauce. Peter watched the clock, while Pat and Danny set the table. Then all were obliged to savor the enjoyable odor of this fabulous concoction for thirty-five minutes. When I tested the flesh of the fish and it flaked nicely, everyone sat down at the table and ate it!

Once a month, I recruited two big kids to accompany me to the commissary at MacDill. We used three carts and worked with precise lists. One of Bob's old friends was assistant manager of the commissary and fancied himself a comedian. He took great joy in announcing over the loudspeaker, "NOW HEAR THIS! NOW HEAR THIS! Ms. DuMouchel is approaching the checkout lines with three loaded baskets! Folks, you'd better beat her to the register if you want to get out of here today."

We just laughed it off, just like we laughed when someone asked us to take their child to live with us for the summer so he or she could learn how to help around the house. We might tolerate a best friend as a birthday treat, or even an occasional overnighter, but the whole summer? No way!

The adults who visited the house, lingered at the refrigerator door reading the laundry schedule, grocery list, and of course, the duty roster. News of our system spread, and we had many curious gawkers, even some strangers suggested, "You need to write a book, Mrs. D!"

Being close to MacDill AFB saved us from driving all over town when someone needed a doctor and allowed us to take advantage of the Sergeant's military benefits - except for Jeff's wart. Nobody noticed when it first showed up on his left hand. He denied ever having touched a frog (so much for old wives' tales). We watched the mysterious wart grow until I couldn't stand it anymore and made an appointment to have it removed. Just two days before we were to go, I noticed the wart shrinking. We had no clue as to what happened. On the day of his appointment, the wart was mysteriously gone, not a sign of where it had been. I called the base and cancelled.

Six months later, the wart reappeared, so I made another appointment, five or six weeks out, because they were booked up so far in advance. For the second time, the wart disappeared before his appointment date. We found it curious, but when it happened a third time a year later, it became a family legend! Whenever anyone had a reversal of plans, they referred to it as being "just like Jeff's wart."

From time to time the girls and I had little "tea parties" and talked about female stuff. After they learned all they needed to know about their physiology, we delved into relationships. One of their favorite topics was their current boyfriends. They had made a pact not to steal their sisters' beaus, something that came easy to them because of our insistence on respect for one another.

While they were encouraged to ask questions, my first response, which became a household dictum, was always, "Don't ask a question unless you're ready to hear the answer!"

"How will I know when I'm really in love, Mom?" Jane wanted to know.

"I've always trusted my instincts, darlin'," I said. She kindly refrained from reminding me that my "instincts" had not served me well when it had come to her father.

"But I will tell you this," I added "Before you decide to spend a lifetime with a man, my advice is to eat with him. Eat with him, eat with him, eat with him! If he's punctual and courteous, that's two good signs. If he's greedy, you'll see it right away. If he's picky and refuses to try new things, that's another clue to his persona. And if he's just plain sloppy or stupid...well, you'll know. Little things will tell you more about a young man's attitude and upbringing than his words ever could. Be on the lookout, watch what he does more than what he says. Don't waste your time with someone who has ugly habits or mean traits. And if you think you're going to change him, forget it! When you get serious about a young man, Honcho and I will ask to meet him. We'll tell you what we think, without telling you what to do."

"One more thing, a reminder to carry with you forever. Answer this for me. What do you do when it's raining?" I asked.

"Run!" Suzi exclaimed.

"Get under shelter!" Leslie added.

"Don't go out without an umbrella!" Kathy declared.

"Right you are! But think about it, girls, when difficulties come, and they will, and you feel confused, open an umbrella. Use your wits, and remember that you have a big family, a team that will always be on your side. Consider each other 'figurative umbrellas', not just to stay dry, but to keep you from getting in trouble. It won't necessarily be a downpour, sometimes just a sprinkle, but you can keep dry and out of a bind if you plan ahead. Consult the brothers and sisters who love you, long after Honcho and I are six feet under." Bob and I felt very strongly about this and he never missed an occasion to instill it in the boys, as well.

Chapter 14

When caravanning grew old, my parents parked their Airstream in our side yard. Dad had researched Ferro cement boats all over the U.S. and was ready to build his own, a 54-foot oceangoing ketch, on our 'football field'. Eventually, they sold the Airstream and bought the little frame house on the other side of the vacant lot and settled into the neighborhood.

I was home alone when a long truck arrived, the driver asking where he was to unload a mountain of rebar and chicken wire. I directed him to the shelter Dad had constructed, high and long enough to accommodate the boat up on blocks. A newspaper article had brought curiosity seekers from all over, and Dad offered those who contributed to the project, either financially or with their labor, passage on the shake-down cruise. Soon the off-duty firemen from the next block and several young men stationed at MacDill showed up and went to work. It also attracted a number of investors.

Jim and Marty Ostrander, from Tampa, financed the $3500 engine. They were also on the job every day. When Dad suggested my mother should feed his work crew, she made it clear that wasn't going to happen. She had no interest in the project and, in fact, was negative about every aspect of his dream. Her open hostility toward those who encouraged him, was a real problem. She often sat in the shade and watched, holding her usual red plastic glass of bourbon and water and her ever present cigarette. But he wasn't willing to give up. He just laughed it off and continued working.

Once the rebar was secured, defining the hull from end to end, chicken wire was layered over the rebar, inside and out; laboriously tied in thousands of places. Then the mixture of Ferro cement, with its high content of silica, was pushed by hand into the chicken wire and smoothed over. He hired our boys as helpers during the summer, nicknaming them 'squirrels' because as the boat took shape, they were easily able to scale the façade and work on the inside where the adult men would have had a harder time. Dad, and the myriad of G.I.s from the base, were forced to climb ladders to the top and then once inside the hull, use shorter ladders to do everything that had to be done. It was an awesome project.

In September, the kids settled in to new schools once again, and Suzi started kindergarten. She carried her shiny new Barbie lunch box, and Peter was careful to keep her in tow as all ten of them crossed two streets, en masse. Since the elementary and middle schools were only a narrow street apart, she was instructed to wait for him after school so that he could escort her home.

It was a little after 2:15 on the first day of school, when I heard the screen door slam and looked up from the biscuit dough I was rolling, surprised to see little Suzi standing jubilantly inside the kitchen. "Whew!" she exclaimed, "I made it!"

We didn't know that the kindergarten let out an hour earlier than the other grades! She had boldly walked two blocks and crossed two streets by herself. Thereafter, I walked the short distance and met her outside her classroom.

After the kids were in bed, some weeks later, we contemplated the things we envisioned for our 'new' old house.

"What about a Dutch door between the kitchen and the dining room?" I suggested. "Would it be a big job to cut the old door in half? Then I could serve from the kitchen, keep an eye on the stove, and still not have anyone under foot."

"One Dutch door coming up!" Bob was already headed for the tool shed, eager to turn my wishes into reality. Despite the late hour, he went to work on the doorframe. I was drying pots and pans and putting them away when I heard him say "Uh, oh," then "Damn!" and "Oh, no!"

"What's that about, Bobby?" I was hesitant to ask.

"Nothing, Suga, I can handle it," was his reply. Finished with my kitchen chores, I settled down with a book.

At midnight, Bob stopped for a cold beer and a cigarette, and stood surveying his predicament. When he had removed the door, he found the hinge precariously screwed into a termite-riddled frame. He called me over, handed me a chisel, and I began neatly chipping at the plaster. One upright seemed easy enough to replace, but, as we went along, each stud proved to be worse than the one before. Seventy-year old horizontal lath supported tons of plaster walls. We began to suspect we were in the middle of a major dilemma.

"What the heck," my eternal optimist reasoned, "that's not so bad. We'll take the whole wall out and have a great big eat-in kitchen."

Bob nodded and then asked, "How many baseball bats do we have?"

"I think four or five." I had to think about that.

"And crowbars?" he asked.

"This one and another in each of our cars."

"Go wake up the children," he decided. "I'll get the tools."

By this time, it was 12:30 a.m. They came down two or three at a time, sleepy, barefooted and grumpy. When we lined them up on both sides of the wall and Bob explained the plan, all eyes popped wide open.

"You guys are going to take these weapons and slam away at this wall. When I say 'go', start trying to kill it." They looked at each other and at us, and Bob started the countdown. On the count of three they started slamming away, wide awake now, still in their pajamas, but we insisted on shoes.

Suzi and Missy didn't have the strength to break up a wall, so I gave them each their little toy brooms and miniature dust pans. The debris was swept into the empty moving boxes we had rescued from the shed. Excitement built, and the noise of cracking plaster and splintering wood was drowned out by shouts, laughter and sometimes songs when Bob started them off. I prayed Mrs. Robinson had taken a sleeping pill.

Each stud was taken out gingerly and the ceiling was braced by the Sergeant Major/Foreman, for fear the second floor would cave in. Then the kids formed a line extending from the work site to the yard, and the cardboard boxes full of plaster were handed off, fire brigade style, through the back rooms and dumped in a pit outside. Unbroken lath was carefully stacked and bound, then reused months later for a beautiful latticework divider to mark off the adults' corner of the porch, providing privacy outside our bedroom windows. Using those original materials provided a bit of nostalgia.

No one took a break that infamous night. When done with their sweeping, Missy and Suzi moved along to standing on chairs by the sink stirring Nestle's Quick into glasses of milk to fortify our team. By daylight, we were all exhausted; our faces were streaked with dust, and everyone's hair was white with plaster snow. We looked around, pointing and laughing at each other.

Breakfast was potluck in the upstairs kitchen, after which Bob showered, shaved, and went to work. The kids helped me clean up, then went back to sleep, smug and satisfied that they had contributed.

Chapter 15

Early in the school year, I was called in to the office of Barbara Leighton, the elementary school principal where I met Mrs. Ryan, principal of the middle school. It seems they had conferred regarding the individual progress of each of the children and determined that some grade changes should be made.

"What are you suggesting?" I wanted to know.

Mrs. Leighton offered, "We have reviewed the records you provided for your ten children, and it appears that those who had the privilege of attending private schools, the children whose name was previously Mouton, are properly placed."

"And the others," Mrs. Ryan continued, "are not as far along, shall we say."

"And what changes are you proposing, ladies?" I was becoming perturbed.

"In all fairness, and to help them catch up, we are suggesting the four others be held back a year." Said Mrs. Leighton.

"Absolutely not!" I was adamant.

"It would be in their best interest, Mrs. DuMouchel," Leighton said.

"No! They have lost their mother, been uprooted to a new community, and they are not to be subjected to what amounts to failure! Give us a chance to work with them at home, and we can revisit this issue after they take their final exams at the end of May."

"Are you going to hire a tutor? That would be an excellent idea," Mrs. Ryan encouraged.

"We have a built-in tutor at home. Two, in fact," I beamed. "I'll work with them and my husband will help me." They were willing to let us give it a try.

Bob and I decided not to approach this as a formal extension of their school day; nor would we single out the four. Instead, including all ten children, we created a variety of word games, read and discussed stimulating books, and held spelling bees. Bob disguised their math lessons by teaching them to cook, concentrating on measurements that had to be doubled or tripled. I had them read editorials in the paper and compose letters to the editor. We made a game out of developing grocery lists and the science involved with managing the fish tank. They did crossword puzzles and became pen pals to improve their vocabularies. Some wrote their own plays, and everyone learned tricks to memorize lines or lists. By the end of the school year, the two principals agreed that no one had to be held back and the children never knew they were being tutored. Win-win.

Chapter 16

Suga, Grandma D, Grandpa D, Bob

A call from Grandma DuMouchel summoned us to Sarasota where Bob's father had suffered a heart attack. We left from the marina the minute Bob closed the yacht basin office, leaving my parents to look in on the children. By the time we arrived, Grandpa D was doing well.

We stayed for a short visit and before heading home, I suggested we add a side trip to Captiva. Jane, Leslie and I had spent an idyllic month there after my hysterectomy and I wanted to share it with Bob. We stopped to see the MacCalls, the Captiva neighbors who had been so kind to us. Bob was eager to see the whole island, so we drove to South Seas Plantation, at the tip of the peninsula, walked around and then went into the lounge for a drink.

A gentleman in a seersucker suit welcomed us, introducing himself as Carter Brown, manager of South Seas. He shared the history of the resort, which was built on an old coconut plantation where they had harvested copra (meat of the coconut) to make coconut oil. We chatted about the weather, which was glorious. Then, to my surprise, Bob said, "Sir, I'm dock master at Imperial Yacht Basin in Tampa," pointing to the insignia on his white uniform shirt, "and I'm looking for an excuse to move to this island." My mouth fell open.

"You have it." Brown replied, "Your timing couldn't be better. My dock master has given his notice and leaves Monday. I'm sure I can meet your present salary. And while we don't usually encourage husband and wife employment, we do have a few couples working here and it's working quite well. There may be a spot for you also if you want to consider it, Mrs. Du-Mouchel."

This was happening too fast for me. I gathered my wits and replied simply, "No I don't think so, we have children." He didn't need the details.

"Just let me know if you change your mind. Now about housing, we can accommodate your family. I have a cottage, used by staff employees in the past. The rent is a pittance and your family will have access to all the resort's amenities." That sealed the deal!

Bob and I looked at each other and silently agreed not to mention how many children we would be bringing, fearing he'd take back his offer.

"How much notice do you want to give Imperial Yacht Basin?" Brown asked.

"Two weeks...?" Bob raised his eyebrows questioningly, as he looked at me, anticipating an objection.

"Well it won't be easy, but I guess I can manage without a marina man for two weeks," said Brown.

The long drive home gave us plenty of time to reflect on what we had just committed to. We'd have to sell Bob's house and mine, plus the one in Port Tampa that we had worked so tirelessly to renovate. We would need to dispose of much of the furniture, and the children would have to change schools again.

In my mind, I began to review the potential problems. Could we come back from a day trip with the news that we were moving to an island? What if the kids didn't want to go? Ridiculous! What if we couldn't sell the houses? Not the end of the world, I concluded; the ones in Brandon and Mango were already rented; and, if we divided the main "funny farm" back into apartments, we would have no trouble renting to Air Force personnel. But Daddy's boat! Good grief! How do you rent a house with a 54-foot half-built boat in the yard? The boys had provided so much help to Dad, maybe he wouldn't finish it if we left!

Bob didn't need to take his eyes off the road to realize I was silently itemizing a list of obstacles. He reached over and squeezed my hand.

"We're going to be fine, Suga," he said. "We're going to be just fine." His sense of adventure was contagious, and he managed to overcome my doubts.

The children were in bed when we got home, and we had a surprise visitor sitting on the porch with Germaine and Bruce. My brother, Jerry, as handsome as ever, dark and mysterious in appearance, but light and friendly in manner, had stopped to visit on his way to Vietnam where he was going to pilot jet planes and helicopters. This was his first opportunity to meet his new brother-in-law and they hit it off right away. We sat up until the wee hours reminiscing, and Jerry told us of his sad farewell to his wife and children in New Orleans as he left for his new duty station.

I pulled out photographs taken on the few occasions we saw each other when we were small. We laughed about the time he painted our grandfather's Packard, and me, in the bargain.

We shared the news of our new venture and, an architect by training, Jerry's main interest was in the structure of the houses on an island subject to tropical storms.

Suga and Jerry

"Go ahead and take whatever you can get, at first," he suggested, "then look around for a piece of property. Let me design a house for you, something unique for my big sister, 'The Old Lady in the Shoe'."

"You know, Bob, you could get arrested for starting a youth camp without a license!" Jerry ribbed Bob as he reached for a pencil and began sketching while I made coffee for the all-night session. Dad had made it clear that he was not at all in favor of this precipitous move, so he removed himself and mother, and they went to their house to bed. I must admit I still had my doubts about the whole crazy idea.

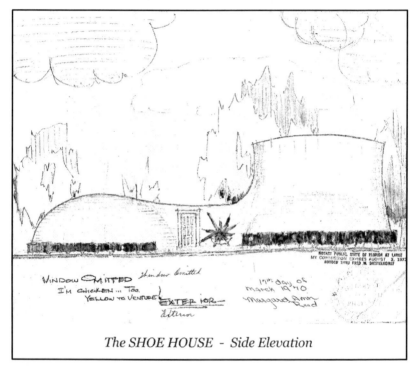

The SHOE HOUSE - Side Elevation

I awakened in the morning to screams and cheering in the kitchen when Jerry revealed the plans to the children. It was fantastic! Bob had stayed up and discussed every inch with Jerry as they shared ideas, and I knew if they said it could be done, we would do it.

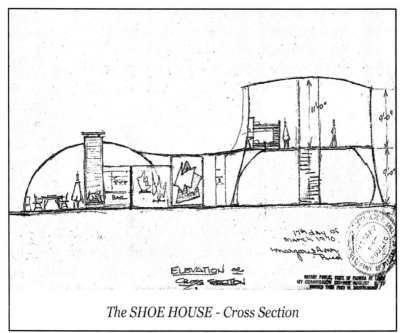

The SHOE HOUSE - Cross Section

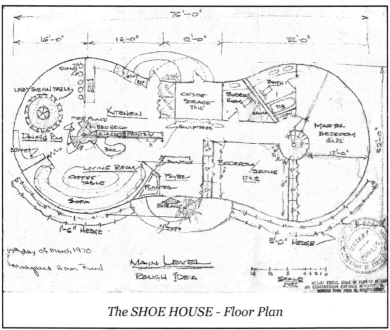

The SHOE HOUSE - Floor Plan

The exterior was to be the same Ferro cement material that Dad was using to build his boat, malleable, to form all contours. Our dream house was to be a huge shoe, with a curved window all around the toe. Inside the toe would be a round settee large enough to accommodate all of us. The round dining table would have a massive lazy Susan. Every piece of furniture was built in. The arch held a giant hearth, visible from both the living room and the master suite, plus the kitchen and the entryway. Our master bedroom and bath took up the heel. Up the boot part were two round dormitories, two baths, and a spiral staircase. He included a firemen's pole from the top, for expediency. Of course, we'd have to sell all three houses to pay for it, but it was unique, we were unique, and we had to have it!

We sadly said goodbye to my warrior brother. He served three times during that siege and, thank God, returned un-scathed.

As if things weren't wild enough, Diana called the next after-noon to say she had been having "little cramps" since early morning. She asked if I thought she might be in labor.

Mike was at work, her father on the golf course with her doc-tor, and her mother visiting in Lakeland for the day. Would I come over and spend a few hours with her?

I drove like a maniac, saying Hail Marys all the way to their apartment. I had only given birth to babies; I didn't know if I could deliver one! Please, Mother Mary, help me!

Diana was as pretty as a picture when I arrived at her apart-ment in Tampa, aglow with pending motherhood. The little cramps were now big cramps, but still twenty minutes apart, so we had plenty of time to get to the hospital; if I could find the hospital.

I alerted Mike's office and left a message for Bob, backstage at the Falk Theatre, to meet me at the hospital between the mat-inee and the evening performance of "Death of a Salesman." Then off we dashed.

Word had gotten to the entire Latino Fernandez clan in Ybor City, and the hospital waiting room was soon filled with what appeared to be every Spanish-speaking grandmother and auntie north of the border.

Silence fell like a pall over the group when Bob arrived in full costume and stage makeup; dressed as Willie Loman's wealthy brother, complete with silver hair, jeweled cane, striped pants, double-breasted vest, stroller jacket, and Homberg. He wore a fake diamond stickpin in his tie and the buttons on his spats shone. The whole affect was awesome under klieg lights, but a bit much in the bright fluorescent hospital lighting. Once they recovered from the initial shock, the grand old Latin ladies "oohed and aahed" and giggled in Spanish. Diana's father followed right on Bob's heels rushing straight from the golf course in his orange and yellow Arnie Palmer-like splendor. It wasn't the first time we had drawn a crowd.

First babies take their own time. Mike needed our moral support, but Bob had an eight o'clock curtain call and I had to feed my litter. We waited as long as we could and promised to return after the evening performance. I dropped Bob off at the stage door, went home, put dinner on the table, dressed hurriedly and headed back to the theater, ready to whisk him away after final curtain. I slid into the box office to phone the hospital. I was pleased to learn that Diane had delivered and was fine; other than that, the girl at the switchboard didn't have any details. Grabbing a young girl acting as backstage gopher, I instructed her to get a message to Bob that his grandchild was born, but I didn't know yet what it was. Then I flopped in a seat in the last row and lost myself in the play.

When Bob made his entrance, I expected him to be relaxed now that the anticipation of the baby's arrival was over, but he was uncharacteristically tight and jittery! I assumed that my message had not been delivered. What I learned later was that she had told him the baby had arrived, but nobody could tell what it was! His imagination had taken care of the rest. Mike joined me at intermission and was thrilled to announce that they had an eight-pound boy! After the final curtain, I joined Bob backstage to allay his fears that we had a monster in our midst.

The final performance of "Salesman" had been a sellout. The audience was totally entertained. We received a call the next day from Vince Petti, the director.

"Bob, you won't believe it! Never in the history of the Falk Theater have we had a demand second run!" he crowed.

"Look, Vince, you know I am leaving tomorrow for a new job. I hate to walk out on you now, but you've put me in a spot." With no understudy for Bob, they wouldn't be able to continue.

"Gee, Bob, I'm sorry if I accepted too hastily, but think what it means to the theater. Can't you call and say you'll be a week late?" He implored.

Bob's integrity was being challenged from all sides. He was torn between his love of the stage, the extraordinary character he was playing to huge applause and big money, and his obligation to a new employer.

He made his decision and called South Seas Plantation. The one-sided, long conversation, I heard, ended with "Well, I understand, no, no, of course. It won't …less money, right, right, thank you, Mr. Brown."

He poured himself a cup of coffee and came to sit with me on the sofa. I wasn't going to ask.

He lit a cigarette. "Smoke?"

"No, thank you," I said.

"Brown's not too happy, says he's had a desk clerk running the marina for two weeks." Bob exhaled on his coffee, watching the steam. My insides grew hotter than the coffee. I was resisting the urge to press him for details. Finally, I caved.

"Bobby! Damnit! What did he say?" This was the kind of game we had played on stage for years.

"Who, Brown?" Bob pretended to be casual and distracted. "Nothing much. He said things were busy. It's the season, you know."

"So?" I attempted to look calm.

"He's going to make the desk clerk his dock master."

"And?" I was tied in knots. We had done so much preparing for the move. What to sell, what to take, what to keep, arrangements with schools, etc.

"He said he has another job for me if I want it. I'm gonna tend bar." He continued, "Now don't get upset, Suga. Its fifty dollars less a month, but I'll more than make that up in tips. I moonlighted as a bartender in NCO clubs when I was in the service, and the tips will be even better in a first-class place like South Seas."

The die was cast. He would finish his run with "Salesman" and then go on to Captiva. The kids and I wouldn't be joining him until school let out.

The plan was to furnish one of the apartments in the Port Tampa house and the Captiva cottage by selecting from the seventeen rooms of furniture plus all we had accumulated from his house and mine. I would then drive my station wagon, crammed with kids, and hire one small moving van for the selected pieces plus thirty-nine cartons of personal stuff and twelve cartons of books and games. Before Bob left, we had sketched every room, plotting and planning down to the last inch.

We piled the 'get rid of' stuff on the porch until it took up so much space that we could no longer access one door. We ran a small ad in The Tampa Tribune for a week and were overwhelmed by the response. It must have drawn a hundred people; some who came to look, some who came to buy for themselves, and some who operated flea market stalls, looking for items for resale. The flea market merchants were a great help in pricing the stuff, but the greatest assistance came from the ones looking for themselves. I was amazed when people asked to buy our empty 48-ounce. peanut butter and pickle jars and over-sized coffee and shortening cans. Average families didn't purchase their groceries in the industrial sizes we bought, so these large containers were at a premium.

We had to dispose of many beds since our 'shoe' would have built-in bunks and the house on Captiva came furnished. Only our antique bed would come with us plus five camp cots we hurriedly purchased. Bob offered a commission to any of the kids who could display enough salesmanship to sell his own bed, or act as a guide for the shoppers. Peter's was the first bed sold. Not only did he get his cut, but he was allowed to sleep on the floor! The rest were wild with envy. Little by little they contrived to sell everything on the porch, except the screen door. Nobody went away empty handed, and many strangers continued to spread the word after the ad had expired.

One caller told me she had heard about our particularly nice harvest table and deacon benches. "Oh, I'm sorry," I said, "they're not for sale."

"I'll pay any price. I just must have that table," she insisted. I had not expected to take the set with us, but, had planned to leave it in the one furnished apartment. After considering what damage renters usually inflicted, I told the woman she could have it and suggested an outrageous price. Her check arrived in the mail, special delivery, paid in full.

On the day of Bob's final performance, I served dinner early to accommodate his 7:30 p.m. curtain call. We had just sat down to dinner when a truck pulled up outside, and a woman and two strapping boys got out. I was hesitant to let them in, but she was in a big hurry to get the truck back. I looked over my shoulder at my family eating at "her" table.

"O.K.," I sighed, "come in."

"Kids," I bellowed, "lift up your dinner plates; Jane, Kathy, please take those serving dishes and put them on the hutch. Leslie, the flowers. Bobby, do you mind?" He looked quizzically up at me, his fork poised half-way between his plate and his mouth.

"Do I mind what?" he asked curiously oblivious.

"Please pick up your plate and your coffee cup." He put his fork down and obliged, agreeably, as he chewed. Everyone pushed their chairs back just a bit, as the woman's two sons lifted the table. I reached out and snatched the tablecloth as it went by, and with one return trip by her boys for a bench, away they went.

Bobby had finished chewing and looked quizzically at me and the children, all standing now, holding their plates.

"I'm sorry, Bobby, I forgot to tell you, I sold the table and the benches." I reminded him our 'shoe' would have a built-in table and big round cushioned seats. Our boys brought a chrome table from their day room upstairs, added two leaves, and we finished dinner.

Chapter 17

We all drove down to Captiva on March 8, 1970, to deliver Bob to his new job. We packed a picnic lunch to share on the beach before heading back to Port Tampa. Captiva looked better every time I saw it, but I was not happy leaving him there and even less enthusiastic about heading back home with ten children, none of whom was of age to help me with the drive.

Our trip was further complicated by the fact that I had an expired brake inspection sticker on my windshield. Therefore, I drove cautiously the entire way to avoid being pulled over. And wouldn't you know it, I got stopped just a mile from our house, near midnight.

"Driver's license?" the policeman said when I lowered the window. I handed it over. He examined it with his flashlight.

"Lady, you have one name printed here and scratched out and another written in!"

"Yes, officer, I did that. I got married last May, but my license doesn't get renewed until next March."

"But you can't do that! And the address is scratched out and another written in. How do I know this is your license?"

"Officer!" I said in mock indignation, "Would I lie to you? Would I lie to him, kids?"

"No, Mama," ten voices chorused. He looked shocked. It was pitch dark and he had not noticed the two rear seats full of children. Suzi had been asleep on a pillow in the passenger seat but was now sitting up and wide awake. He ducked down, looked into the back with his flashlight and counted heads.

"Where are you going with all these kids at this hour?" he demanded.

"Home to put them to bed. These are all my children. We just drove their father to work five hours from here."

"You have ten kids and you just got married in May?"

"Twelve," I corrected him, "two aren't here. What? You think I kidnapped ten kids?"

"I take my hat off to you, lady. Go get that inspection sticker tomorrow and I won't give you a ticket. And take these kids home and put them to bed. God bless you."

As was my practice, before I turned the key, I began our litany aloud with: "One, two," (for Mike and Steve, who weren't with us), Danny then shouted "three," Pat said "four", Eddie "five", Peter "six", Kathy "seven", Jane "eight", Leslie "nine", Jeff "ten", Missy" eleven", and in her sweet little musical voice, Suzi said "twel-ve" in two syllables. This was the system I used to make sure I hadn't left anyone behind.

"And good luck!" The policeman smiled and shouted as I started the car.

Good luck, indeed! The boys were adrenalized and couldn't stop talking! Even I had expected to get hauled in for altering my license, if not for the expired sticker. The little girls either didn't comprehend or didn't care.

The next morning the kids went to school as usual. The house felt empty without the Honcho, but I was bound and determined to carry on as though he were here, and I knew he'd insist I get the new inspection sticker. I went out to the car only to find I had a flat tire. Thank you, Blessed Mother, for being with me so it didn't happen on the highway last night between Captiva and Tampa! Dad saw I was in distress and changed it for me.

Three hours later, after waiting in the hot sun, in a maddeningly slow line, my car passed inspection, and a sticker was applied to my windshield. I left the inspection station and was on my way to see my grandson, Jason Michael, when I got hopelessly confused on Hyde Park's one-way streets, a fancy neighborhood near the hospital on Tampa Bay. I found myself headed God knows where.

The car ahead of me stopped at a stop sign and as he moved on, I heard the high whine of an approaching ambulance. Pulling over onto the gravel shoulder, I waited for it to pass and then went on my way, turning left in an attempt to get my bearings. Two blocks farther a patrol car flew by going in the opposite direction. I had my confounded sticker, and no further need to hide from the law, so I waved bravely and was properly ignored.

Within a few blocks, I heard what I presumed to be another ambulance. In my rearview mirror, however, was what I thought might be the same patrol car. Its blue light was flashing, so I pulled over and stopped. The officer got out and sauntered over like an arrogant cowboy, his big black gun catching a brief glint from the sun.

"May I see your driver's license, ma'am?"

Instead of reaching for it, I said, "You're not going to like it. You see, I just got married and my license isn't due for renewal yet, so I wrote in my new name. I've also moved, so I corrected my address, too. All of which I've recently been told I'm not supposed to do, but nonetheless, I have already done it. Now, last night a policeman let me off because I have twelve children, but I can't take them with me everywhere I go, just to keep out of trouble." I smiled, hoping to lift the mood. "And I have a brand spanking new inspection sticker and I haven't done anything wrong, so I suggest you go about your business and I'll say goodbye and be on my way."

"May I see your driver's license?" He repeated louder.

"I just told you about it."

"I still want to see the license, lady." He was rude. He was probably constipated. I handed him my wallet, flipped open to show my license, and he copied something from it. Then he tore off a flimsy piece of paper and handed it to me. Was this a ticket? I had never been given one in my life, so was not even sure what one looked like.

"What's this for?" I demanded. I was annoyed, hot and lost, and this Hyde Park policeman didn't give a hoot.

"You failed to stop at a stop sign back near the hospital," he alleged.

"That's not true! I stopped in the gravel for an ambulance to go by, then I went when the coast was clear."

"Hey, lady, I'm not going to stand here and argue with you."

"My youngest son calls me that." I quipped.

"Calls you what?" he asked. Before I could explain that Jeff nicknamed me that back when he couldn't remember my name, but that was no longer important because now he calls me "Mom", the policeman recited, as I am sure he had many times before: "If you don't think you should have to pay the fine, you have the prerogative of asking for a hearing at which time you can tell it to the judge." I was at full attention now.

"How much is the fine?" I asked in a humble voice.

"I don't know that. You'll have to go to the courthouse anyway, they can tell you. Goodbye!" He started back toward his car.

"Wait!" I cried. "Please help me, I'm lost!" I was taking a chance that he would extend some human kindness to me, and I must admit, he was a gentleman and escorted me to Mike and Diana's address.

When I arrived, the baby was asleep and while I waited to see him, we had coffee and I told Diana about my adventures with the law.

"Don't pay it," she said firmly. "It's your first offense, right?" I nodded. "The judge will probably let you off with a warning. If you pay it without protest, it's marked on your record and noted on your license. If he lets you off, you're free and clear."

"What do you mean the judge? Are you seriously suggesting I should go to trial over a stop sign?" For an intelligent person, there were areas in which I was seemingly born yesterday. This was my daughter-in-law, my friend, having to advise me about traffic fines.

When my court date arrived, I took Pat with me. He had stayed home from school, recovering from the last remnants of a bad cold. I couldn't leave him home and take the chance my parents would find out I was going to court. Pat had started shaving recently, at the tender age of thirteen, and looked mature than his years. I hoped people would think he was my casually dressed lawyer.

We sat in traffic court for two hours listening to one dreary account after another. It wasn't at all like trials on "Judge Judy". It was boring and consisted mostly of mumbled conversations between the defendants and the judge. He was handing out sentences like lollipops and making everybody go to safe driving classes. I was afraid I had come on a day when he was in a bad mood. Pat was enjoying it all but had to keep running out to put money in the parking meter, as I had parked in a thirty-minute zone. I had given him my last nickel when my name was called.

I felt even smaller than my five-foot two inches, approaching the towering judge's desk. There was a long table on my left surrounded by seated policemen, and a half-dozen lawyers were grouped around another table on my right. There I stood, alone, like Joan of Arc.

The judge asked my policeman to read the charge. It sounded formal and fancy the way he described my car, the time of day, the direction I was headed and his position at the time. It was at that moment that I had my first inkling that I might get out of there alive.

The judge then asked me if I had counsel, but Pat wasn't back yet. I answered in my best courtroom voice, "No, your eminence. I shall represent myself because my lawyer just ran outside to put my last nickel in the meter. I have a few opening remarks; may I approach the bench?" I think he was impressed.

"Your honor, sir. First I must tell you the incident in question happened on the first day and the worst day of my life." He was really interested now. He said, "What?"

"It was the first day of my life because I have twelve children and my husband had left the day before." He had, technically. "And it was the worst day because I had to wait three hours in one of your abysmal inspection stations for my brake sticker. Now. I would like to call as my first witness, the arresting officer."

The buzz of conversation at the lawyers' table stopped and they all turned to watch. They seemed to be impressed, too. The policemen looked amused.

"Young man," I said to my officer after he was seated. "How old are you?"

"Twenty–seven," he answered cautiously, not knowing where this was going.

"I see. And what kind of vision do you have?"

"Twenty-twenty." He looked queerly at me.

"I see. Now would you please tell the court what special capacity you have for seeing around right angles."

"What do you mean?"

"No further questions," I said dismissing him. "Go back to your seat."

"Your honor, sir," I addressed the judge. He leaned way over to see me. "May I utilize that magnetic board over there with the little cars on it? I would like to make a point."

He instructed someone to bring the board. It had streets painted on it and I removed all the magnetic cars, except one, which I placed at an intersection.

"Now, this represents the car that had been stopped in front of me on the street described as "headed north" by this astute young policeman, whom, I might add, was really nice to me." I hoped his commanding officer was in the courtroom that day and took notice of the fact that I was commending him.

"He helped me find my daughter-in-law's apartment where I was going to see my first grandson, after he gave me the piece of paper that turned out to be my first ticket. Ever! In my entire life! I would like to make it a matter of record that he helped a lady in distress. Now, here's where it gets good. This red car is me, I drive a red Ford station wagon. I was also headed north." I placed a red one behind the first car.

Using both hands, I said, "This car stopped and then proceeded across the intersection, at which time I began my approach to the stop sign. That's when the siren of an ambulance prompted me to move off the road, thusly. I stopped about three feet short of the sign, in the gravel, to let this" and I zoomed another little vehicle around my corner, "ambulance pass." I held up a little paneled truck and promoted it to ambulance. "Got that?" The judge nodded.

"After it was gone, I turned left, which is east, crossed the big boulevard and went two blocks before I saw this policeman's car coming." I positioned a blue car on the board at exactly two blocks from me.

"He passed me, by his own admission, going west. Young man, how fast would you say you were going?"

"About thirty miles an hour." He just cooked his goose. It was a fifteen-mile zone!

"Your honor, sir, don't you see, that at the time I pulled off the shoulder to let the ambulance by, this officer was blocks away. He simply could not have known that I had stopped around the bend, at the stop sign within clear sight of the street and oncoming traffic. He was coming this way and saw my front end approaching the corner from the gravel. He assumed that I had not stopped at the sign. And, by the way, by his own admission, he violated the speed limit, but we'll overlook that."

All the while I was talking, I was maneuvering little cars to describe the situation and my brain was racing ahead for a sensible way to conclude. I couldn't remember the phrase, something Perry Mason says when he's finished talking, and I was grasping for the right words when my spiel ran out. So, I turned with a flourish, faced the judge, and with both hands gestured grandly and said, "Case dismissed!"

The lawyers howled, the policemen started laughing, and even the judge chuckled on his bench.

"No!" I cried, "Wait! I'm sorry! That's not what I meant!" I turned to a woman whom I assumed was the court reporter.

"Strike that," I said to her, "I meant, the defense rests!" But she was doodling on a Kentucky Fried Chicken napkin.

I was petrified. I looked over, somewhat consoled that Pat had returned, but he had pulled his golf hat down over his face.

"Young woman," the judge said when he composed himself, "you've impressed me. You presented your case admirably. I agree with you that the officer could not have seen what you had done around a blind angle. However, I will suggest that in the future you pull all the way up to a stop sign before proceeding into an intersection. I encourage you to drive with caution at all times. Case dismissed."

"Thank you," I said humbly. I turned and walked out past Pat, who still wouldn't acknowledge me. I backed up a step and stopped right in front of him tugging at his hat. "Come on, Pat," I said, "we won!"

Chapter 18

Bob had been in Captiva for only a few days when he phoned and asked me to drive down, alone, for the weekend to take a look at 'Lime Grove', the house Carter Brown had offered us The house was just a mile down the winding road from where he worked in the lounge. Traditionally, it had been occupied by the manager, but Brown was single and preferred to live in a simple hotel room near his office. I was blessed with good weather and parents nearby who would look after the children.

Bob fumbled with the lock, in the dark, and snapped on the light once we were inside. I followed him into the big, glass-enclosed porch we would use as the boys' bedroom. The girls would share the large bedroom, Bob and I the smaller one. Then he led the way into the living room, complete with a sofa that opened into a bed. The sides of the sofa and chairs were woven cane, with attractively covered cushions, impervious to kids, sand and salt water. The dining table was large enough, but I made a mental note to bring extra chairs from home. The kitchen was modern and quite adequate, leading out to a porch in the rear, big enough for the freezer; a happy surprise. There were lots of windows everywhere, covered with sheers. It was a modern Florida house, and it was air conditioned.

While I took my bath, Bob whipped up a cozy little candle-lit dinner of steaks, salad, and a bottle of Chateau Le Dominique. It was extraordinary for us to be dining alone. He had a lot to tell me about his job. He enjoyed tending bar and had been right about the tips being great. As it turned out the hours were perfect. He had two hours to fish before he went in at eleven, and when he had the five o'clock shift, he could play eighteen holes of golf in the morning.

As we ate, Bob began a campaign to have us join him sooner than our agreed upon summer break. "Why delay?" he wanted to know. He said he needed his big family around him and we could move during the Easter holidays. All I had to do was drive back to Tampa, he said, pack up and haul the children to the island. That's all, I mused?

I hesitantly relented. I would be relieved to get away from Dad's endless negative rhetoric about making the move. I had already informed my customers and completed my sewing commitments. I didn't need Bob to help me sell the rest of the excess. I knew I could wrap this up alone, after all I had overseen every relocation since Jim and I left New Orleans in 1957. And now I had twelve young people to help, no babies or toddlers anymore!

The next morning, after Bob left to inventory his bar, I was alone in my new kitchen with a stack of dirty dishes. I laughed out loud at the stack, compared to what a stack of dishes was at home in Port Tampa. When two cereal bowls plus silverware and coffee cups were washed, dried and put away, I put on my bathing suit, grabbed a towel and a book and headed for the beach. I stopped long enough to appraise the exterior of what was going to be our new home. It had redwood siding and white shutters and was nestled in a shelter of exotic shrubbery, barely visible from the road. Pink, yellow and flaming red hibiscus grew roof-high on all four sides, interspersed with sea grape and small palms. A tall row of wild green things I couldn't identify grew at the edge of the road.

There were two ways to get from the house to the beach, either around a bend on the hot sand road, or through the jungle in the back yard. The latter would bring me about thirty yards farther onto the Plantation grounds, where I was likely to find privacy. The public was not allowed on the resort's beach, and being a mile from their accommodations, the guests would be unlikely to wander this far.

I chose the jungle route which grew right up to the clearing that was our back yard. I boldly stepped into the leaf-matted no man's land. My bare legs were the first to suffer the folly of this decision. Spanish bayonets grew wild; every imaginable thorn bush lurked nearby and the ground, in places, was soggy and oozed mud. I jumped and twirled, expecting to sink in quicksand. I could see sunlight through the leaves, so the Gulf could not be more than fifty feet away. I could smell it.

My towel got hopelessly entangled in the thorn bushes. Ripping it loose, I had to brush aside a family of large spiders to retrieve my book which had slipped from my hands. I had been slapping at gnats and mosquitoes all along; and looking down to avoid roots and holes, I saw that my legs were covered with pests. I fought them fiercely and wrapped the towel around my legs for protection, no doubt trapping many of the varmints against my lower body.

The branches above were a worse menace. I should have kept the towel on my shoulders as defense against sharp and brittle mangrove branches and the multitude of spiders. I had begun my journey upright, but as I went on, the jungle grew denser and I was forced by vines and branches to duck and stoop into a crouched position. Between slapping at bugs and picking my way among thorns and twigs, I stepped on something that streaked away in the underbrush before I could register what it was. My imagination took over and I grew desperate.

Here I was in my own backyard enclosed in a wet, green tomb, probably a mangrove swamp. I could yell my head off and no one would hear me. There were no houses past the MacCall's and ours for a mile. Calling for them was hopeless, they had air conditioning, so they would not hear. Plus, they were old and frail and couldn't help me.

There was no standing still to ponder my predicament. I had to keep moving to outrun the mosquitoes. I couldn't even think about snakes, leeches and small varmints, or I would go mad! I peered ahead in the direction of where the beach was supposed to be, but the sunlight was no longer there. I was completely turned around, with no landmarks by which to get my bearings. There was nothing but more and more dense, green thicket.

The only clearing in sight was over my left shoulder, another ten yards to go unless my eyes, now squinted closed, deceived me. Perhaps, I needed to turn and move west. But, why? Since I didn't know what direction I was headed when I started, it wouldn't make any difference. I was in tears. Angry and frustrated with the bugs, I was scratched or bitten on every inch of my body not covered by my bathing suit.

My imagination and self-pity took over. How would my children feel when they learned that their mother had gotten lost in the backyard and died in that jungle? What if my body was never found? Bob would think I had gone swimming and drowned. He'd probably drag the whole Gulf of Mexico! I had to get out of there! Slap...slap...scratch, sob...scratch.

Hallelujah! As I shoved aside yet another leafy bush, I saw my house! A few more steps and I stumbled out, popping up in the backyard! I wanted to throw myself down and weep under the clothesline, but the mosquitoes were having a grand banquet, having sent word to all their friends to come devour this idiotic, tasty woman.

I ran frantically for the house, nearly wrenching my right arm out of the socket when I jerked at the screen door. It was locked! Making a dash for the other side of the house, a swarm of buzzing insects trailing in my wake, I found the front door locked also! It must have locked automatically when I let it slam. What could I do? Across the street, Bernice had no doubt opened her gift shop by now, so I couldn't interrupt her customers. I shouldn't...but what choice did I have?

Dashing wildly across the street through ankle deep, hot, powdered sand, I burst into her cool and immaculate shop. Three tourists in crisp, lovely pastel Bermuda shorts, sun hats and dark glasses, were looking around. They gawked at the mad woman in the bathing suit who panting and scratching in the most unladylike places.

"Bernice," I sobbed, "please excuse me…I'm sorry!"

Needing no explanation, she came around the glass showcase and led me, scratching and hopping, through her shop and into her apartment. Mac, sitting at the kitchen table tying fishing lures, looked up, peering over his glasses.

"Mac," she stated calmly, "Lynne has gotten into the mosquitoes, take care of her." He must have played this role before, because he nonchalantly opened the back door and led me out to his yard without a word. For some mysterious reason, there were no mosquitoes there. He turned a hose on me, full force, allowing me to luxuriate in a fierce stream of cold water, the drops mingling with my tears.

"One other thing," Mac said with a straight face when he turned the hose off, "this island has a lot of mosquitoes."

$$\backsim \,\mathcal{X} \backsim \,\mathcal{S}$$

Back in Tampa the following week, I completed my final shopping spree at the commissary and base exchange. The last item on my list was a case of 6-12 Insect Repellent. The kids were not going to be imprisoned in the house when they had the full use of the resort and the run of the five-mile-long island.

I then put a blurb in the Brandon paper. It said, "SEAN MOUTON DUMOUCHEL NEEDS A HOME." Many people who knew us, called wanting the details, but not the Great Dane. He was well loved, and it grieved me to let him go. We had been told that employees could not have animals over 24 pounds, and Sean weighed many times that. He was terribly crippled with arthritis, but I could not have him put down. I was too much of a coward to watch him die.

We had only one taker, Molly Dickie, who offered a good home for him on her farm in Pinecrest. She had an aging female Great Dane who needed companionship and agreed to care for our poor old Sean.

I couldn't bear to see him leave, so when Molly came to claim him, my mother handed over his rabies records, bowls and toys, his lawn spike and his chain. The kids had said a tearful goodbye to him before they left for school.

Coincidentally, many years later, I was to encounter Molly at a barbecue in Pinecrest. She had a beautiful brindle Dane and I began to share my story of how Sean cared for the children and me. She told me that she had also had a dog named Sean, whom she got from a big family in Port Tampa. She said he was reputed to be smart, but he was the dumbest dog she had ever seen. When given commands or called for his meals, he only stared strangely at her. Germaine apparently, had failed to inform the lady that Sean was from Belgium. We had always spoken to him in French, the only language he understood!

Chapter 19

I got the children ready to leave on Good Friday. My dad helped pack the car, still muttering about how much he disagreed with the move. Taking the kayak Bob had built, we filled it with small boxes and last-minute odds and ends, placing it on top of the station wagon as a carrier. Daddy assured me that it was secure. The top of the car might come off, but the boat wouldn't. Trust a nautical man to tie good knots, any sailor worth his salt was trained in marlin spike seamanship! I prayed all the way up to the pinnacle of the Sunshine Skyway Bridge, where we had to make Danny hide his eyes because he was terrified of heights. We were leaving St. Petersburg, and, so far, we had lost neither boat nor roof.

Encountering a driving rain in Sarasota, we rested at Grandma and Grandpa D's house. When the rain didn't slow up after an hour, I decided to reload the kids and continue to Captiva in the waning daylight. After Grandma D's homemade pies, cakes and coffee, I was ready to face anything. Or at least, I thought I was.

Darkness was approaching as I drove straight through Ft. Myers, paid the three-dollar toll onto Sanibel, and saw, for the first time, what effect a downpour could have on a low barrier island. While Sanibel was populated and had a drainage system, Captiva was little more than an inundated sand bar in the unrelenting rain. Armed with only my gumption and my headlights, I went on blind faith that the road was there between the two rows of trees standing in water.

Though I was terribly frightened, I couldn't let on to the children how precarious our plight was. After traversing the twelve miles of Sanibel, and what I estimated to be about four miles on Captiva, I knew it couldn't be much further. We couldn't be lost, Captiva was only five miles long and had only one road with South Seas Plantation at the very tip of the island.

I thought that, surely, I'd see a light in Bernice's shop any minute. Blackness surrounded us, and the tires were making loud, slushy sounds in the deep water. There was only one street light on both islands, and we had passed it long ago at Bailey's General Store on Sanibel. Then, through sheets of rain, blowing branches and threatening palms, I caught sight of what appeared to be a light on the side of the road. It was Mac, in an orange slicker waiting for us in the rain, with a lantern dangling at his side! God only knew how long he had been there.

He helped me find our deep sand driveway and avoid plowing right ahead into the gulf. We shouted our thanks as I led the way through the yard, unlocked the door, and hustled the children into the house, wading in water up to my shins. Danny carried Missy and Suzi, one under each arm. Pat held Jeff on his shoulders, and Eddie hefted skinny little Leslie on his back through the flooded yard. Peter, Jane and Kathy managed to slog through by themselves, closely following the big boys in the dark. Water poured into the dark house during the time it took to herd ten kids through the entry. It was no surprise to find we had no lights; electricity didn't stand a chance on the islands in bad weather. Well, we would just learn to live with candles and lanterns. Maybe the kids would consider it an adventure, I thought, undaunted.

I felt my way through the pitch-black kitchen, to the cabinet where I had seen Bob store his flashlight. I shone it around the room until the light landed on my ten drenched children, exhausted, but happy to be out of the car. The stress of driving through the storm had taken a toll on all of us. The car could be unloaded in the morning. Everything in the kayak, now filled to the brim with water, was already ruined.

The children had devoured their packed sandwiches and snacks during the long trip; followed by cake and cookies at their grandparents' home in Sarasota. I had nothing for them at bedtime, but they didn't seem to mind. I showed them to their rooms and the bathroom. The girls fell into their beds, boys on sofas, leaving soggy clothing on the floor.

I sat alone in the dark at the kitchen table, cold and uncomfortable in my wet clothes, pondering how we were going to live with only one bathroom, mosquitoes, temperamental electricity, and no telephone.

Suddenly a worse realization crept in. Bob had gone to work at 5 p.m., I assumed on foot, since his motorcycle was on the porch. We had no way of letting him know we had arrived safely, and I was afraid he might attempt to navigate the treacherous mile along the beach, waist-high in churning water.

I had no choice but to drive up to the Plantation. We do what we have to do, fortified with faith in God and adrenaline. I waded out to my car, praying the distributor cap hadn't gotten wet. It started, miraculously. Struggling through the water for a mile on curvy, unlighted roads, I reached the high gravel ground at the entrance to the Plantation. Approaching the parking lot outside the restaurant and bar, I gave no thought to the way I looked. I slipped in through the back door and felt right at home among the soaking wet, newly arrived patrons who mingled with the brocade and sequined gowns of the ones who had arrived earlier. Bob was happy to see me and proudly introduced his "gutsy" and bedraggled wife. I stayed until the end of his shift and although the water hadn't receded, Bob was able to get us home safely. He had been concerned about our making the journey in the treacherous weather, but said he never doubted for a minute that I'd make it. I appreciated his trust.

I learned, in time, that tropical storms were seasonal and seldom dangerous. The mosquitoes were seasonal also, fortunately. We learned to drink the sulfur water, smelling like rotten eggs, from our faucets, as advised, and the no see ums and mosquitoes stopped biting us, moving on to the tasty tourists. The heat was intense for only a few hours each day, until replaced by the gulf breeze in the afternoon. Since electricity was erratic, kerosene lamps were part of every island home. We had a telephone, but called it 'object d'art', since any call off the two islands imposed a toll charge. We cherished our new life of privacy and peace.

There were only fifty-five children in the elementary school, and ten of them were ours. We had one or two in every grade from first through seventh. On their first day, the school bus picked them up at our door, and when the ninth one boarded and the bus had pulled away, I discovered Suzi standing by my side, holding on to the tail of my shirt, sucking her thumb. I had forgotten to register her! "Oh, my God!" I said. "Get in the car, baby." I fastened her shoes while she buckled herself into her car seat. I sped the few miles to the school and found Mr. Runnels, the principal/math teacher/janitor, waiting for us in the parking lot.

"I knew you had one more," Runnels said. "I saved a place for her."

There was another family with six children and an even bigger family with fourteen and that was the entire "minor" head count on Captiva, all of whom rode the bus to and from school and in no time had formed strong friendships.

The children loved the island, learning to walk up the slanted palms like natives, eating coconut meat with their hands after a good chop on the hairy shell with a machete. Everyone turned pink, then tan. We made clam and coquina chowder from the bounty we found in the shallows, dug oysters out of the shell banks, caught fish and netted crabs from the piers. All this largesse was plentiful, fresh and delicious.

I drove to Ft. Myers once a week for staples and convinced the bread truck driver and the milkman to make our house a regular stop after calling on the chef at the Plantation. Our freezer was on the unlocked back porch and each delivery man knew which shelf was for milk and which for bread, so they kept them filled and just left a bill.

The children swam daily, rarely wearing real clothes unless they were going to church. Jeffrey always kept special sea shells in his pockets, for tourists bending over looking for treasures. He would offer them to the ladies, who refused at first, but when he explained that he lived here, they always rewarded this generous little boy with dollar bills.

Many evenings, we enjoyed picnics on the beach rather than eating at our table in the house. We bought a seine net that the kids and I dragged through shallow water up to the beach, collecting living wonders to fill our salt water aquarium. Eddie became the authority on marine life and we all learned about tropical birds and plants with the help of our set of encyclopedias. Eventually, the kids made money working as bellhops, bus boys, dock boys and errand boys. In no time, Leslie had a babysitting service for guests of the Plantation, and Kathy and Jane each worked at the gift shop in the summer. Missy and Suzi boldly approached Mr. Brown, asking for a job that six and seven-year-old ladies could do. He offered them each, fifty cents a day if they would keep cigarette butts picked up from the grass around the swimming pool. But it was, once again, Jeffrey who proved to be the most enterprising, when he collected baitfish by the bucketful and sold them on the dock to fishermen for a quarter a piece.

Pooling their money, the boys bought a couple of mini-bikes to drag race on the grass airstrip at the south end of the Plantation, directly behind our house.

Bob bought a little twisted cigarette for the two of us to sample. We waited until the children were in bed and their lights off, locking our bedroom door. He tried it first, then handed it to me.

It didn't taste like anything at all, but what did I know? We didn't feel any sensation, but maybe we needed to give it more time. After a few minutes of puffing away, the smell brought Pat, Peter and Eddie knocking on our door.

"Hey, whatcha doin' in there?" Pat asked. We heard them whispering and giggling.

"Nothin'. Go back to bed," Bob ordered.

"Come on, Dad, I think you're gonna get into trouble, let us in."

"Go back to bed, kids, we need a little quiet time. You're not invited."

"Mom are you smoking pot?" It was Peter.

"I smell it, Mom, let us in." This was Eddie's voice. Bob handed me the little cig, pointing toward our bathroom. I took it with me, closing the bathroom door behind me. He told the boys emphatically to go to bed, then he joined me in the bathroom.

"They won't smell it in here. I should have thought of that in the first place. Where is it?" he asked.

"I flushed it! Sorry. I thought that's what you meant when you pointed to this door!"

"Well, so much for that."

We were all invited, along with the Bissell family, to sing at the Sanibel Community Center Christmas program. Don Bissell, father of the other six blondies on Captiva, joined forces with Bob to teach all sixteen kids to sing in three-part harmony. They trained them, with no semblance of acoustics, out in the open on the beach, sitting on felled palm trees. This went on during all of November and the first two weeks of December. By that time, the men realized where the best voices were, and it was suggested, kindly, that Peter should only move his mouth, silently.

Just before we left for the party, Bob was called to work, so the kids and I went without him. The show must go on! Ginny Bissell and I were invited to appear with the children when we arrived for the festivities. Ginny was about my size and age, also wore short blonde hair, and we had on similar blouses and skirts, quite by accident. We could have passed for sisters. As a matter of fact, Don stood between us on the stage, and, being very new to the island, no one could figure which of us was his wife. The kids were all so similar in appearance that the locals were not able to identify which kid went with which mother. There was much speculation and curiosity over punch and cake, but we made no effort to help. The performance was well received and the whole program considered a resounding success, according to The Island News.

Chapter 20

Since we had arrived, Bob worked many long shifts, sometimes with no free time for weeks on end. Finally, during the
slow season, we were advised to take a break and Paul Stahlin,
Jr., son of the resort owner, looked after the kids for us. We took
this opportunity to drive to New Orleans for a week, visiting
Aunt Rosie and Grandmother Moore. On that Saturday, my
cousin, Betty, and her husband, Dave Cambre, hosted some of
our aunts and uncles for lunch. Uncle Lee brought my grandparents from the nursing home in Slidell. My grandmother had de-
mentia and neither knew where she was, nor who I was.

Proudly, I introduced Bobby to my family. There had never
been a divorce or remarriage in my Catholic family and I was
apprehensive about what would be said about my second husband. But everyone was courteous and fascinated to have an actor in their midst. Their conversations were peppered with
questions about celebrities Bob may have encountered throughout his career.

Papa Sarrat asked Bob what he did for a living now. "I'm a
bartender," Bob said nervously, knowing he was in the company
of high society. "Oh, son," my aristocratic grandfather said,

"I'm so happy to hear this! I consider that to be one of the most noble professions!"

Bob and I toured the French Quarter the next day, stopping in at Pat O'Brien's for one of their famous Hurricanes, served in a tall souvenir glass. We had a jazz lunch at the Court of Two Sisters, then dinner at Antoine's. He wanted to see the aboveground cemeteries the following day, so we walked into St. Louis Number II on Esplanade Avenue and I showed him the massive stone tombs where the Sarrat and Michel ancestors were buried. In the distance we could hear Pete Fountain's trumpet call to the post. It was the height of racing season at The Fairgrounds, less than half a mile away.

I showed Bob where I had grown up, just thirty paces off Bayou St. John. He was surprised to see a bayou right in the middle of a city filled with cobblestone and paved streets; not at all what a person from Michigan would expect. We strolled on the small levee, where my mammy, Amélia, had walked me to elementary school in the early 40's.

The Sarrat House, now on the National Registry, is fronted by DeSoto Street with Hagan Avenue running along the side. One stipulation of the National Registry is that the façade of a structure must be preserved regardless of changes made to the interior, just like the buildings in the French Quarter. Just a few blocks down Hagan is the famous Parkway Bakery, where we got juicy roast beef Po'boy sandwiches to go. I insisted we should get some to eat on the way home when it came time to return to Florida at the end of the week.

We sat on the grass to eat our Po'boys at the water's edge in front of the landmark 1799 Pilot House, a Creole colonial home, also now on the National Registry.

Bobby questioned the heavy, rusted rings firmly embedded in cement, placed strategically along the four miles of the bayou's edge. They were installed along a manmade concrete walkway a mere twenty inches wide. I explained that the rings, about ten inches in diameter, had been used to secure boats that came from all around Lake Pontchartrain. For generations, farmers and merchants, tinkers and tailors sold their wares and practiced their trades from small boats along the bayou. Today Bayou St. John is free of boat traffic, generally enjoyed only by kids jumping off the bridges to swim.

On the last day we packed up and thanked Aunt Rosie and Grandmother Pauline for their hospitality. We stopped at Parkway for our Po'boys and then headed home.

Returning happily to our family, they bravely recounted the blackout they had experienced one night. It seemed that some of them made the most of the darkness by putting sheets over their heads and terrorizing the smallest kids. All of which only upset and antagonized our sitter. Missy, Suzi, Leslie, and Jeff admitted they had fun playing along.

In no time at all, Bob was made bar manager. Danny, Pat and Peter moved from bus boys up to waiters and Eddie became a bellhop. Bob then had control over his work schedule and our lives settled down to some degree of normalcy.

One day, Carter called me into his office to ask if I could work a few hours a day performing clerical duties, plus help Bob out by cashiering on busy nights. Since all the dinner checks had to go through the cash register in the bar, it was a hassle for one man to serve bar customers, fix drinks for thirty tables in the dining rooms, plus operate the cash register. Keeping a second bartender had proven to be nearly impossible. It was a revelation to us that service personnel were highly transient, moving with the seasons to places where the tips were better. Some of these bartenders were also quick to dip into the till, so they were fired before we learned their names. As a result, Bob sometimes worked seven days a week, twelve hours a day. Don't misunderstand, he surely didn't mind the money, nor the added benefit of a captive audience, which he entertained with his repartee!

So, I went to work. I typed a few letters, took reservations and learned to check guests in and out, sort of a floating right-hand woman. More often than not, Bob also wanted me to cashier when he was off, so I could watch the other bartenders. It proved to be a lot of hours for me, but pleasant and relaxing. He was delighted to cook for the family and enjoyed being a househusband; keeping up with the laundry and monitoring the kids on the beach. I was very happy to have no sewing deadlines and no dance lessons. Of all my duties, I much preferred serving as cashier for Bob's shift. We completely debunked the theory that husbands and wives could not work together. Our tips were so good, that we could just bank our paychecks.

There were five other couples, husband-wife teams, spread among many departments. When payday came with a full moon, half the single staff went "down the road", and they abandoned us en masse during hurricanes, leaving the six couples to hold down the fort. We made salads when the electricity failed, served tables, changed beds, met incoming guests on the airstrip and loaned out our cars during the gas crunch.

The search was on for our own piece of land, but we soon learned that Captiva residents were wary of newcomers. Their fear was based on what happened on Sanibel as it developed commercially and lost much of its unique charm and privacy. The only way to control things was to hold on to the land and enforce strict building codes. Our plan to build a shoe house was outrageous to the old timers. One customer at the bar, who worked for Life magazine, claimed that if we built it, he'd get the magazine to pay for it. We certainly would have taken that offer if we could have bought a lot, but it was futile.

There was only one service station on Sanibel, none on Captiva. Therefore, it was subject to long lines of tourists and residents waiting to get gassed up. Little Jeff jumped on this opportunity. He took our big (we had nothing small) thermos filled with coffee, Styrofoam cups, and with his own money bought bags of donuts. He would then load up his red Radio

Flyer wagon and traipse up and down the long lines of cars sell-ing 'breakfast'. He made out like a bandit.

When Mariner Group, seven young entrepreneurs from Mich-igan, bought South Seas Plantation, they kept all six married couples on to maintain the status quo and had us teach them how to run a resort. While they possessed business acumen, the hotel business was new to them. Alan Ten Broek and Bob Taylor, the major duomos, were our friends in no time. Bob often sang their special love songs when they brought their wives in for dinner. Tommy Yeaser, the resident musician, knew all their favorites and accompanied Bob on his guitar.

And oh, what we learned from the professional waiters! They could size up a customer before he sat down. Exchanging looks, they could identify a shack job, a big tipper, a roué, and they taught Bob and me how to recognize these types. Funniest of all were the bored to death, long-married couples, those folks who had run out of things to say to each other. One night, our favor-ite waiter, Jose, told me to get close to a certain table to hear what was being said, or not said. The man said, "A B C" and his lady smiled sweetly and responded, "D E F G," to which he asked, "H?" She shook her head and within seconds took up a new subject, smiling, "1 2 3 4" and he interrupted with "5 6!" and so on and so forth.

One memorable Saturday afternoon at the Plantation bar, to break the monotony of a long day, Bob walked around to the big picture window where he could watch our kids carrying on in the swimming pool. He boasted to the drinkers nursing after-noon beers, that he had a good mind to go outside and throw one of those noisy kids in the deep end to shut them up.

"You wouldn't dare!" a big Swede replied, not knowing, of course, that Bob was looking at his own children.

"Just watch me." He went out and stood innocently poolside for a moment, and when skinny little Leslie dashed by, he reached out to toss her! I came around the corner of the building just in time to see good old Dad climbing out of the pool. A soaked, limp cigarette dangled from his lips and water poured out of the sleeves of his spiffy red bar jacket. Our forty-five-pound Leslie, whom we called "Skinny Minnie," had held on to Bob's lapels and dragged my handsome husband into the water with her. The lounge was filled with laughing, roaring customers, golfers and fishermen, many of whom had come in just in time to witness this turnabout.

The big Swede's face turned bright red, and he said with gusto, "I told you so! From now on your name will be 'Bob-in-the-drink'!" They called Charlie Feirich, the dock master, 'Charlie Overboard' because he so often fell off the dock.

During the off-season, the resort capitalized on conventions. South Seas booked one or more per week all summer into November. We especially enjoyed the Cadillac group which filled our island with pastel and gold Cadillacs. Of course, at the bar they drank a cocktail called 'Golden Cadillac', though many changed the name to match their cars.

The convention of school teachers was lively. Railroad men, dentists, bird watchers, sales groups and stocking manufacturers each had unique characteristics and charm. We made and served more than a few new friends.

To expedite checking in dozens of people at once, I found a way to alleviate the slow check in and luggage pile up at the reception desk. I simply came out of the office, climbed onto their tour bus and registered everyone in their seats while handing out keys. The driver had a map of the grounds and delivered them to their doors. Eddie and the other bellboys missed out on tips but made up for it later.

Our days and nights were filled with an ongoing parade of unforgettable people, and that included the celebrities. The Plantation was a favorite escape of many famous people, being at the tip end of an island with no thru traffic, no press watching and no phones in the rooms back in those days. We honored everyone's privacy; no one on the staff asked for autographs or photos and this allowed our illustrious guests to feel at home.

I found myself face-to-face with Elizabeth Taylor, Lucille Ball, and Vivian Vance, among many others, and never flinched.

Bob was delighted when David Niven joined him afternoons at the bar, exchanging stories and sharing some of his verbal tricks.

George Sanders would sit at my desk when he was bored and just seemed to enjoy watching people check in and out. He was greatly amused when one guest, upon leaving, refused to pay the additional dollar per day for her dog because, she claimed loudly, "My dog didn't have a good time!" With a straight face, I let it slide, removing the pet charge from her bill. To me, pets were less destructive than children; I never saw a dog write on a wall with a crayon!

However, it was the pediatrics convention that was most memorable. It leaked out that the bar manager and his wife, the cashier, had twelve children. Any time either of us served drinks in their private dining room, we were greeted with a standing ovation from the baby doctors, and great tips followed. Peter learned to capitalize on this when he waited tables; telling the doctors that he had hoped to have a career in medicine, but being one of twelve children, he didn't stand a chance. That sob story brought fifty-dollar tips to the resourceful seventeen-year old.

There were many occasions when our island residents contributed to the full and interesting lives our children enjoyed. One who comes to mind was a little old man, a Russian hermit who lived in a one room shack across from The Island Store. He was pleasant with the children, extremely formal and respectful toward me. One day he showed up at my back door and handed me a faded old satin bag filled with foreign coins.

"What's this, Mr. Osmin?" I asked.

"Please call me Basil, ma'am."

"And you can call me Suga, Basil. It's a nickname I've had all my life. What do you want to show me in this fine little bag?" I inquired.

"It's many coins from Russia for the children. I wanted your young people to see them and divide them up, keepsakes for them, from me. Tell them about the interesting countries they might learn about in school, places from my side of the world," he explained as he extended the bag toward me.

"Basil, if this is your personal collection, I can't take it. It must be valuable."

"Please, take them for your children, it will make an old man happy," he insisted.

"Thank you, Basil, I'll see that they cherish your gift." We learned a few days later that he had died. When his little house was razed, the land owner put up a crazy restaurant on that site, "The Bubble Room." It is still there and very popular with everyone, especially children. An electric train runs continuously on tracks about a foot below the ceiling and travels, tooting and puffing, upstairs and down, throughout every room, including the bar.

Robert Rauschenberg, a famous artist, lived around the next curve. He was renowned for his sculpture-painting hybrids known as combines. We got to know him well, as he sat at the bar most afternoons drinking scotch and milk. He invariably forgot where he had parked his dusty little Volkswagen, and one of us would have to take him home.

His house had previously been owned by a ship captain's widow, Clara Stran. For over 20 years, she had run the Stran Shell Shop out of the house. Collectors came from all over the world for the Shell Fair every March and Clara often exhibited her prizes in the community building. She would poke her head out and talk with me anytime I walked past, going to The Island Store. She loved hearing about the children's antics, as she had none of her own. Clara informed me that the old islanders and retirees were beginning to refer to the kids as "our children."

One day she invited me to come in and sit down. Jeff had become her favorite and she had hired him to pick up her mail for her. Clara told me she had concluded from their conversations, that Jeffrey didn't understand that his mother had died.

"But, Clara, he was so little, he doesn't even remember her," I told her.

"That's the point, Suga, he needs to be taught about death," she said.

"Maybe when he's older his dad can have a talk with him."

"No, I'll take care of that," she said firmly, and changed the subject.

Later that day, I found myself reflecting on what Clara had said. I then recalled that shortly after our wedding, Bob had found Jeffrey peeking through our bedroom keyhole with a flashlight, always on a Sunday morning. Over and over, he talked to him, even spanked him when he gave no reason for snooping on us, but the next Sunday he did it again. Finally, through angry tears, Jeff cried, "Dad, I have to! One time, on funny papers day, the first mother was gone! You told me she died and went to heaven! I need to be sure this one doesn't leave, Dad!" I decided Clara was right.

The following day Jeff came in after school and calmly told me he had gone to Mrs. Stran's with her mail, but he found her on her bed and she was dead. He said it simply, with no agitation. He said he figured she had died when she was going to bed because one of her stockings was off. Then he went out to the beach to swim with the other kids. I dashed over to Mrs. Stran's house, after notifying Paul Stahlin, our Island Commissioner, and he took charge of the situation. Clara had personally, gently, and effectively taught Jeffrey that death is simply a fact of life.

Some months later, Bob and I both had the night off and planned to spend the evening at home with the children. It was a quiet, dreary night and we were shut in by dark clouds, thunder, and rain. The TV wasn't getting a signal and Bob asked, "Who wants to have a séance to communicate with Mrs. Stran?" The kids all made spooky sounds and laughed nervously. When a candle was lit in the center of the table, they gathered round, some sitting, some standing. The lights were turned off, then Bob started in a loud stage whisper, "CLARA STRAN, CLARA STRAN we are your friends who want to visit with you tonight."

Missy interrupted, "Er… Honcho."

"Not now, Missy," he whispered.

"Honcho," she said louder.

"Not now, Missy," he repeated. He started again, drawing out her name, "C..l..a..r..a."

"But, Honcho," she insisted. "Please, Honcho," Missy cried once again to his annoyance.

"Missy!" he said abruptly. "Go to the bathroom, if you must."

"No, Honcho," she cried plaintively, "your chair is on my foot!"

Before Bob could move his chair, Peter let out a champion-level fart that cracked up the whole group and the séance was over.

Chapter 21

An old itch had found us in our island home, the desire to go on the stage again. Sanibel had a little theater, the Pirate Play-house, but the offerings for the 1970-71 season were one-act or original plays, and we weren't interested. Bob was ready to do a heavy, professional drama and had been talking about it for over a year. Comedy would be fun, but we could really sink our teeth into a good drama. With good writing, it's easy to make your audience laugh, but we both knew that if you can make your audience cry, you've really got them.

"Look at this," he said, one morning over the newspaper, "the Actors' Repertory Theatre is auditioning for "Cat on a Hot Tin Roof," now that's my kind of show! Tennessee Williams doesn't write silly little comedies. It calls for 'five men, three women, two Negroes and five children'."

"Children in a Tennessee Williams play?" I asked.

"Do we have a copy in the house? I'd like to read it," Bob said.

I went to our bookshelf and searched the volumes of plays. It was in a fat black book which I took down and handed to Bob. He looked it over and said, "Tomorrow night, I'll get Ralph to tend the bar and I'll take his shift. We're gonna do this play!"

"Which of the children are we going to take?" I wondered out loud.

"They don't specify ages, let's take them all, that way we're bound to have the right age kid."

It poured the next day. Undaunted, we drove thirty-five miles into Ft. Myers, found the audition hall, and lined the children up. I prepared them outside, "Now please, remember who you are. You've all been around theater people; you will be quiet while anyone is reading for a part. If you are given a chance to read, we expect you to do your best. No giggling or whispering. Jeffrey, go get a drink and go to the bathroom as soon as we get inside, then come sit with your brothers."

Bob led the way and I followed him into the building. Suzi was right behind me and the rest were lined up like ducks in a row by size, up to Danny. The girls all had on summery print dresses, made from the same material as mine. We might not get roles, but they would know we were there. A young woman was reading lines as we stepped inside the door, so we hesitated until she sat down.

The director, a small wiry fellow with an infectious grin noticed Bob and me in the doorway and motioned us to join the rest of the actors awaiting their audition. When we walked all the way in, followed by ten children, and took up two rows of seats, the director took off his glasses.

"Well! What have we here? Look, everybody, the first dinner theater production in Ft. Myers has just been cast!" Everyone in the room chuckled and a kind lady asked Bob, "Are they all yours?"

"You have to be good at something!" He answered proudly with a strategic pause while people tittered and laughed. His timing was flawless. "My wife is deaf, you see," he said, "and every night when we go to bed, I ask her, 'You want to go to sleep or what?' She always answers, 'WHAT?'"

He had them in the palm of his hand. When they stopped laughing, we listened to the next hour of auditions without stirring.

"Let me have someone read for Big Mama, please?" the director ordered.

"Go on, Mom, you read it," the kids egged me on.

"Come on, mother," the director encouraged me. "Can you read this with a southern accent?" I was disgusting, I was so southern. The children applauded, and I gave them the look.

"Fine, thank you," the director said to me, "I'd like you to read the part of Mae for me now. She's the sister-in-law, younger, selfish and bitter, a kind of bitchy type." Then he asked for volunteers to read the part of Mae's husband at the same time. No one spoke up, so he handed Bob the playbook. "Can you read a few lines and let me see how your wife relates in conversation?"

"Sure," he said. We had just read a few lines when the director stopped us.

"Waaait a minute! You've done this before," he said to Bob, his eyebrows arched high. "I have a better idea. Can you pull out all the stops and give me age sixty-five? I want you for my Big Daddy."

Burl Ives had played Big Daddy on the stage and in the film. I didn't see my handsome husband as Burl Ives, but he could be padded and grow a beard. The room fell silent as he began a soliloquy in the blustering Big Daddy voice. I had chills when he finished. The director was shaken. He wiped his brow and extended his hand, "My name's John Wyatt."

This was the beginning of a marvelous, profitable friendship. Bob got the lead, our four youngest, Jeff, Leslie, Missy and Suzi, were chosen to play the children, and I was cast as Mae. Bob took the day shift at the bar and we drove in to Ft. Myers each night for three consecutive weeks for rehearsals.

Bob became Big Daddy, huffing and yelling in his newly acquired southern accent with such power, his performance was riveting. Being the first dinner theatre production held in Ft. Myers, "Cat" drew attention from all over the state and on opening night the capacity audience was peppered with dignitaries, local celebrities, officers of the Florida Theatre Conference, plus many old friends. When Big Daddy was on stage you could hear a pin drop. He fumed and cursed and threw his son, Brick, around the stage. He sweated and cried, and the audience cried with him. He hated all the bratty children of his oldest son and "that bitch, Mae" and when the children and I were throwing lines at him, he was vehement in his pseudo dislike of us.

I had trepidations about the children losing their composure when they realized how close the audience was going to be. Ft. Myers had no theater, so the staging took place in the huge dining room of the Sheraton. In theater-in-the-round, you can reach out and touch the nearest table, but these kids kept their cool and not once allowed themselves to be distracted. They were satisfactorily obnoxious, as Tennessee Williams intended them to be. Being a southern bitch was second nature for me, and the greatest compliment I received on my performance was from Elaine Patton, daughter of General George Patton. She came to me after our premier and said, "I just hated you…you were marvelous!" The newspaper reviews were outstanding.

I began to suspect that God did not plan for us to have simply a plain and boring life. I was not meant to "sit still and look pretty" as Jim had advocated.

On one memorable night, in the middle of one of Big Daddy's blustery speeches, Bob's false teeth got loose and nearly made it out of his mouth. With great effort and a quick gesture with his right hand, he managed to keep them from getting away. The audience responded immediately. They clapped enthusiastically at the near faux pas, and John Wyatt loved it, begging Bob to repeat it each night. But he refused, knowing how disastrous a slip would be if he lost them on the floor! Who could argue with him? They were his teeth.

Toward the end of the play Big Daddy, finds out he's dying of cancer and has a scene to end all scenes. The play was interrupted night after night with thunderous applause on his last exit. The big moment came when the final scene ended, and we joined hands for the curtain call. The minor players accepted their applause, then the rest of us and the kids received well deserved applause, but when Big Daddy came out, the audience went absolutely wild. They rose to their feet, applauding and whistling. Policemen kept them from overwhelming us, the audience screamed "bravo" and clapped some more. We couldn't get off the stage. Bob was overwhelmed and cried with humility and pride. If he never did another play, the triumph of that moment was enough to carry him for a lifetime. And I feared he would not be able to do another play. His cough was frightening.

We had taken rooms at the Sheraton beginning with the last week of concentrated technical and dress rehearsals because the thirty-five-mile drive, each way, every night was too much. When the show opened, we kept the four kids out of school for the month. Many of their teachers had seen the opening of "Cat", so our little actors were met with true excitement upon their return to class.

Suzi came bouncing off the school bus and ran into the house on the first day they were back.

"Mommy! Mommy!" she called out, "you know what a celebrity is?"

"It's sort of a disease some actors get. Why do you want to know that, baby?" I answered.

"No, no! I know what it is! It's a little girl with her front teeth out, 'cause today my teacher clapped when I got to school, and she said, 'Here comes the celebrity!'"

While it was tempting to work again with the repertory theater, we had to put our family first. As time went on, we also recognized that the three-hour bus ride each way to middle and high school in Ft. Myers put the older kids at a disadvantage. They were missing all after-school activities. They couldn't play sports, join a club, go to a dance, or even attend a function. Jane, Kathy and the four oldest boys were being deprived of an opportunity to socialize with their peers. They had their jobs at the Plantation but were not enjoying their teenage years.

Drugs were readily available on barrier and coastal islands, and some of their friends succumbed. We were wary. I had made a friend of Sgt. Walter Pulumbo from Ft. Myers, who came out often to check on liquor regulations and occupancy counts. He promised to alert me when his men planned a drug raid. I would then mention it to our teenagers, sometimes when it wasn't true; a white lie that I hoped kept them out of trouble. Hopefully, if they had any contraband, they would dump it and warn their friends.

One day, I drove into Ft. Myers to look for new material at Clothworld. I stopped for a traffic light, and to my amazement, there was Pat, sitting at a bus stop, alone, when he should have been in school! He was just as surprised to see me, and when I rolled down the window and invited him to get in, he did so, willingly.

"Good morning, Patrick," I said sweetly. "May I ask what you're doing waiting for a city bus?"

"Gee, Mom, you're the last person I expected to see." He cast his eyes down.

"And may I ask where you were going?" I gently asked.

"I couldn't stay in school today. I was going to get out of Ft. Myers and hoped to hitch up to Michigan to Aunt Lorraine's," he admitted.

"Pat, you like school. Why are you running away? Tell me, please, maybe I can help."

"No, Mom, this year I don't like it. I have the hardest subjects first thing in the morning, when I'm not alert. I just started hating school and didn't know what to do."

We went to MacDonald's, and over a cup of coffee and some fries, he gave me an earful. He was going through some normal teenage angst, and I thought of a possible solution.

"Pat, would you mind coming with me to talk with your guidance counselor and let's see what she might have to say?" He agreed, and she was concerned about Pat's disenchantment with school. I told her of the times Pat had shown such creativity when he helped the little kids with posters, and how he helped me each season when I painted acrylic scenes on our windows for holidays. I asked if there was an art class that was early each morning. There was and when she got him into it, his whole attitude toward school turned around.

But as time went on, even though the kids managed to fit into island routines, Bob and I seriously weighed the pros and cons of taking them back to the real world. Living at a resort is something less than normal. A family conference proved us right. They voted unanimously to give up beach life for city life.

By mid-December we were back in Port Tampa and the kids renewed old friendships. The boys helped Gramps again with the boat, Bob went back to his old job at Imperial Yacht Basin, and I returned to the sewing machine; all of us better for our island experience.

Chapter 22

Bob came home from work the night after Christmas with a miserable cough and a light film of perspiration on his brow. Rarely sick, he was battling some form of the flu. He was physically fit, a former Golden Gloves contender who rigorously maintained his fighting weight, ate carefully and worked daily with his speed bag mounted on the ceiling and a jump rope. His only weakness, his incessant smoking. On this night, he sprawled face down across the bed, still wearing his yacht basin uniform. After tucking the youngest children in, I came downstairs, and grabbed a book before propping myself next to him.

Sometime later, knocking, no banging, on the front door startled me. Shocking, because it had been such a quiet night.

"I'll get it, go back to sleep," I whispered to him. I was still dressed, and hurried to the main entry, the banging had not let up. Flipping on the porch light, I opened the door and was surprised to see a frantic, middle-aged man. He shouted, "Anybody upstairs in this house?"

"Yes, why? My children…" I stammered.

"There's smoke and flames coming out of the attic, ma'am you've got to get everyone out!"

"Twelve, no, ten children!" I blurted. Without another word, I turned abruptly to the stairs with the man following me. At the top landing, a blanket of smoke hung a foot above the floor.

"Oh, my God! Where is the fire?" The man reached my side and entered the first room as I turned and ran back down to wake my groggy husband.

"Bobby! Bobby! Wake up! There's a fire!" He looked at me with unfocused eyes.

"Where?"

"Upstairs! Smoke is everywhere!"

"Fire? In the house? What are you saying?" He was beginning to understand.

"You've got to get up and help me get the children out! Grab the blanket, it's freezing outside!" He struggled to his feet and followed me with ever increasing speed as I went back up the stairs, both of us shouting, "Fire! Everybody up! Fire!"

I ran into Danny, bounding down, barefoot, in a T-shirt and shorts. "Mom! A strange man woke me up. He said there's a fire!"

Behind me, Bob ordered, "Danny, call the fire station!"

Danny launched himself out the door and started running toward the fire house, just a block away. Bob leapt up the stairs two at a time and disappeared into the darkness, just as the stranger emerged from the smoke carrying one of the girls, cradling a fancy pillow in her arms.

Once outside, the stranger ordered, "Stay here," calmly setting her down on the grass before turning back to the house.

The three of us spent the next few minutes pulling sleeping children out from under their blankets. I knew I could only carry the small ones and headed first for them. The smoke inside grew dense and it became increasingly hard to see anything. Two of the boys, Pat and Peter, met me on the staircase.

"Mom!" Pat said, pointing to the room they had just vacated, "The smoke is too thick, don't go upstairs. Where's Dad?"

I ignored him, pushing into the room where the three oldest girls slept. After rousing the coughing eight-year old, Leslie, I sent her down the stairs, going back to the youth bed where Suzi slept. I carried her out and handed her off to one of her older sisters in the yard.

The children stood trembling on the sidewalk holding on to each other, uncharacteristically quiet, their eyes fixed on our burning house. They watched as Jeffrey climbed out a window, scurried across the porch roof into a tree, and then dropped to the ground. Something he had been told so many times not to do.

Sirens shattered the quiet night. Two huge, red engines pulled up and men in yellow turnout gear jumped out and ran toward the inferno. Nearby houses were spattered with red and blue lights from the police vehicles, that spun around and lit up the night. Lights and noise created a surreal scene on this usually quiet street.

Neighbors, wrapped in blankets and robes, came out of their homes, approaching from up and down the block. In the shadowy darkness everyone seemed to be milling around.

"Count them! Please help us!" I didn't recognize my own hoarse voice. I counted out loud, "They are five, six, seven, two eight-year-olds, two ten-year-olds, two twelve-year-olds and Danny, fourteen." I had recited that litany from the first day our families had been joined. But I realized they were older than that now! I can't think! How old? Where are they all?

I had gone back in but could no longer find the smaller children, while Bob and the stranger brought the bigger ones out passing me on the stairs. We could barely see where we were going, stumbling. Dashing back into a bedroom, shouting at two boys to hurry out, I yanked a quilt onto the floor, opened a chest of drawers and tossed anything I could grab in the dark onto the quilt, pulled the four corners together, then headed down the stairs with the awkward bundle. I was met by a monstrous, roaring ball of fire; an updraft that knocked me clear off my feet. The huge load ignited and blew up and over the railing, casting flaming clothing into the air. At that point, I hugged the wall while firemen pulled a hose up the stairs. I tried to grab one of the men to get his attention.

I cried. "Please count them, there are ten here! I'm not sure we have all of the kids!"

"You need to get out, ma'am," a firefighter insisted. He all but tossed me down the staircase, past unrecognizable shapes and figures; another guided me out the front door, literally pushing me out onto the porch.

From outside, flames illuminated the entire building; inside, there was no seeing through the thick, putrid smoke. I had always called on my senses to get around in the dark, able to find a drowsy child's doll, or a favorite blanket without turning on a light. Tonight, I needed to find our children.

I was frantic, I couldn't think straight. "One, two, three, are they here? Four...who's missing? Jane? Where's Jane?"

"I'm here, Mom". I heard her but couldn't see her in the milling crowd.

"Danny? Suzi? Missy? Kathy? Jeffrey?" I screeched.

"I don't know where Jane is," Kathy called to me, "but I have the little girls, Mom!"

"Is there anyone else?" The firemen asked.

"Yes!" I shouted. "More children and Bob. Where's Bob? Where's my husband? I'm going to get him!" I fought to get past them.

"Ma'am, we have men in there, they'll bring him out." They held me back. I heard pounding footsteps, unfamiliar voices shouting indecipherable words.

"Help us find the children, please!" I cried, begging the men going in. Some of them carried heavy axes; others pulled a massive hose into the fire.

"We'll get them, ma'am, how many more?"

"I don't know! I don't know! Maybe some ran back for something! Where are all the children? I don't know where they are! I can't count them!"

An isolated voice said, "The neighbors are taking them into their houses, ma'am, to get them out of the cold. It's thirty-two degrees out here."

On the sidewalk in front of the house, concerned neighbors were sobbing. We watched through a window in horror as the huge Christmas tree in the foyer sizzled, and ornaments and bulbs popped and exploded. Drapes, upholstery and rugs flared upward in red and black fury. I backed away into the street. Then I saw him. His face filthy with soot, Bob walked through the crowd and wrapped me in his strong arms. Tears streaked his face.

"Bobby, are they all out?"

"I don't know, Suga, they won't let me back in."

I fainted. I awoke on the cold wet grass, Bob hovering over me.

Violent flames flashed out the windows and a shower of sparks rained onto the corrugated tin roof of the wraparound porch, adding to the overwhelming noise. People gathered around us and spoke to me, but I couldn't grasp what they said, nor did I recognize faces. I struggled to see our children in the darkness, but all I could see was smoke billowing up into the night sky.

"Bobby, have you found all the children? Where's the man who helped us?" I begged.

Bob hugged me, and a neighbor threw a thin blanket over both our shoulders. A silent scream filled my head, louder than the crackling and crashing noises coming from the house only a few yards away. Why does fire make so much noise? How can everyone just stand here? Why isn't anyone bringing out more children? It's going up too fast!

A line of firefighters, paramedics and police officers blocked the sidewalk next to the house, now nearly half destroyed and caving in on one side. Bob and I moved back across the narrow street with the rest of the crowd. Filthy, shocked, and dumbstruck, we watched the holocaust; both of us believing some of our children had perished. We remained silent for fear that saying it would make it so. There were no stepchildren, they were all ours and forever would be. Neither of us had stopped once to consider which ones we carried out.

It was daylight before we could gather the children in my parents' house. The fire chief attempted to count them, over and over. The poor man struggled, because the children moved constantly, the big ones shuffling the smallest ones from one lap to another and wrapping them in welcome arms.

"They're all here, all ten kids, whew! Do they ever sit still? How do you do it?" he asked, to lighten the moment, grinning.

"Just like everyone else, only more so," Bob said. His laughter caused a hard round of coughing. The smoke hadn't done his lungs any favor.

The chief addressed the exhausted adults, "I have to ask you folks, do you have any enemies?" We stared back, dumbfounded. We had fans, but none of us had ever heard of an enemy.

"Enemies? No, sir, we have no enemies. Certainly, no enemies!" Bob responded. He then offered his hand to the fire chief. "Thank you and all your men. We thank you." His tears fell silently.

"We'll find out how this started, but it may take a few days." The chief was confident.

We watched as the last fire truck pulled away from the dripping, blackened mess that had been our home. The house where, just two nights before we had a joyous Christmas party. Bob stood across the street looking up at the remains of the house he loved, the hulking skeleton we had spent two years and every spare cent restoring. I joined him.

"Bobby, YO?" (our code for "you ok?")

In a hoarse whisper he said, "Yes, Suga, now that I know you're all safe, I'm thinkin' about how we'll rebuild." He put a loving arm around me.

A gentleman from St. Patrick's, our parish church, came to offer assistance. "Tell me what you need. Tell me what we can do for you."

The children had spent the first night sleeping on their grandparents' floor. I looked around at their bare feet and soot stained pajamas. No one had a toothbrush, a comb, or even a sock. We could no longer claim a pot or a dish or a change of clothing. Every piece of furniture, every bed, pillow, and every clothespin, all gone. I was numb, and in response to his question, I thought, "everything." We needed everything, but I didn't speak it.

Through my parents' window I could see the charred frame of our home. The maple Early American china cabinet, a remnant from my life with Jim, was a skeleton of blackened, warped boards. I recalled happy earlier days when we had filled the shelves with precious crystal stemware, wedding presents, a service for twelve. The front glass panes on the doors were now all cracked but the lovely glassware stood proudly on those shelves, undiminished by the terrible heat.

Why hadn't someone turned on a light? And who was the good Samaritan who had helped us and disappeared before we could thank him? Focus, Suga!

I turned to the man from our church who was so patiently waiting. He showed no embarrassment when tears trickled down my face, matching similar tears on his cheeks.

"Shoes," I said simply. "Can you please find some shoes to put on these children? Their feet are cold… and they have no socks."

"I'll see what I can do. I didn't realize it was so bad. I'll be back tonight."

Reaction to the first box he gave us brought out the natural enthusiasm of children over anything unexpected. They pulled out clean folded sheets, an assortment of clothing and a stuffed Snoopy, which was automatically handed to Suzi. Each child put on something; Missy chose a man's thick flannel shirt with its tail dragging the floor. We laughed when she strutted like a debutante in her first formal gown.

Bob and I went to sort through the smoldering, sopping black debris.

"Is it safe to go inside, Bobby?" We stood on the first step.

"The chief cautioned me, but I think part of the second floor is holding better than he expected. Do you want me to take you in?" I nodded. I had on two of my mother's sweaters and her boots. We were surprised, at first, to see the porch intact except where the firemen had taken the doors off to get their hoses in.

"Watch out for the glass, the windows are all broken," Bob warned.

The front door, half glass, where Pat and I had painted a nativity scene before Christmas, was cracked right down the middle. Mary and Joseph on one side, the baby Jesus, lambs and a shepherd on the other.

I stepped gingerly around charred debris tossed out by the firefighters. One small mattress still had a fitted sheet on it, badly singed around the edges. The sheet was smoked marble gray except for the white blur in the middle where a sleeping child's body had lain. I stood fixated, staring at the silhouette of Suzi's little body, wondering why she hadn't been covered.

Once inside, I felt strangely disassociated as we waded through ankle-deep water, kicking aside floating picture frames blackened with soot, and bits of charred wood. The stench was overwhelming. Shreds of soaked, colorless cloth hung from a curtain rod in the living room. I stared at it for a moment before I realized it had been a fiberglass curtain that had melted.

My eyes traveled slowly around the room; a wall that had been solid book shelves was a mass of dripping pulp. Bob had built shelves floor to ceiling on four walls, to hold our collection of books, all ruined now. The skeleton of the Christmas tree bobbed in the water, weighted down by its stand. Bobby took an axe to the floor in the middle of the room, letting a deluge of water pour out through the hole.

A heap of red wax was melted on top of my white piano; a Christmas candle? Soggy plaster from the ceiling covered the blackened keys and I carefully scraped aside as much as I could before I closed it for the last time. Bitterly cold water seeped through our shoes and chilled us to the bone. The kitchen trash can had toppled over; remnants of our twenty-two-pound Christmas turkey carcass floated across the room. Gifts melted into each other and Eddie's drum set was charred. He had begged for this gift for years, and we had finally managed to buy it for him. Leslie's toy sewing machine was burned beyond recognition.

"Suga, the only important thing is that we're alive," Bob said. "We can replace material things." He reached for a stringy melted plastic mass atop the sooty refrigerator. "What do you suppose this was?"

Red letters on plastic rounded bubbles spelled out "AFT." I recognized it and a sob strangled my voice, "Marshmallows," I whispered. "Kraft marshmallows. I made cocoa for the children last night." He held me close while I cried.

We had done dishes together the night before and placed our wedding rings on the kitchen windowsill. He pulled debris out of the sink but found no rings. There would be no recovery after the force from a fire hose.

"You are so strong, Suga. I'm weak in so many ways," Bob admitted. "I feel like I've let you all down."

"I've seen enough," I said. "The kids can't think we're defeated, we need to go reassure them."

"Suga, let's go back and count them again." He led me back out. It was freezing.

That afternoon I assembled all ten children outside, under the boat shelter, each wearing hand-me-downs they had pulled from charity boxes. Some had shoes and socks that didn't match. Making them hold hands in a circle, I stood in the center, gathering my courage.

I looked sadly at them, tears choking me, using the familiar countdown I used when I was about to start the car. "One, two," I began our routine using the numbers of the absent biggest boys. Danny said "three", Pat had trouble speaking, but called out his number after a beat or two, saying "four." Eddie swallowed a sob, saying "five," Peter followed with "six," Kathy quietly said, "seven." Jane perked up and said with spunk, "eight!" Leslie had a tremor in her voice when she called out "nine," followed by Jeff's "ten," and in a little voice, Missy said, "eleven." An even smaller voice closed with Suzi's sing-song, "twel-ve." I took a deep breath, savoring their full attention for a moment.

"We're all here. Look at me, you guys. We've lost our house. We've lost our clothes and shoes, our books and furniture. But listen carefully to me. Have we lost everything?" I asked. Ten solemn, dirty faces nodded, some said sadly, "yeah," or "yes, Mom."

"Now, I want you to look at each other. Check out who you're holding on to and who's holding on to you. We have each other. This…is all," I swallowed a sob, "you will ever need." We pulled together in a group hug and Honcho stepped over and put his arms around us as only he could.

We never saw the stranger again. I wrote a letter to the editor of the newspaper expressing our thanks to the good Samaritan.

Chapter 23

For a week, food came from neighbors. There were trays of fried chicken, bags of sandwiches, candy bars, and a grocery sack with cereal, eggs, and milk; generosity we couldn't believe.

After a newswoman interviewed us in my folks' living room, and described our predicament on TV, boxes came from various sources. One oversized Northern tissue carton arrived brimming over with odd socks. The girls got busy matching up sizes and colors. Kathy was jubilant when she showed me what she had found, "Look, Mom, we're not so poor. We have five pairs of socks that match, and we'll wear 'em even if they don't!"

About noon the second day a car pulled up as I stood across the street looking up at the cupola on the destroyed roof. A stout, dark haired woman got out. "Are you the mother of the children who lived there?" she asked, handing me a large carton.

"Yes." I didn't recognize her.

"I saw your family in 'Cat on a Hot Tin Roof' in Ft. Myers and I want you to have these." She unloaded two more boxes from her trunk.

"Thank you. Who are …?" I attempted to ask.

"God bless you." She got back in her car and drove away while I stood transfixed.

That same generous lady came back several times; she had collected a truckload of contributions for us, including a washing machine. She introduced herself as Grace Young, from Brandon. In the weeks that followed, we became friends. She encouraged me to write the story of our wedding and the fire and offered to edit it for me.

"I'm a step ahead of you; I have a few chapters already typed. My folks were reading it when the house burned, so it wasn't lost in the fire." I told her.

While we were performing in "Cat" I had been provided with an assistant who made up, dressed and monitored the kids, getting them to their entrances at the right time. That left me not only free, but idle, stuck in a dark hall where I waited for my next appearance. I decided to use that time to write our story. I would sit on the floor with a yellow legal pad and a pen, a small flashlight in my mouth.

Years before, when the children were very little, Grandmother Moore had visited us in Atlanta and shared her personal, scandalous background. She told me she trusted me to write her story, but not to publish it until after she was gone. When I mentioned this to her daughters, some years later, they said, "Oh no, not until after **we** are gone!" I could wait, and now I had more to write. I had been given a beginning, and the DuMouchel story could now be added to it.

Mike, Diana, and Steve had collected all sizes of clothing, plus household odds and ends. Boxes continued to arrive, and the boatshed filled up with washing machines, sewing machines, furniture of every description, and enough dishes and tableware to outfit us, plus one more burned out family. Bob and my dad salvaged parts from contributions to make several workable appliances. One extremely generous donor brought ten backpacks filled with school supplies.

When the insurance adjuster offered to put us up in a motel, my immediate fear was that no motel would take ten kids. I found one in nearby Brandon, taking three rooms directly over each other. Bob and I took the ground floor, the five girls directly above us, and the five boys over them. That way if they stomped around, only our family would hear it. We ate in the hotel dining room and shopped at Goodwill for appropriate clothing, so they could start back to familiar schools after the Christmas break.

The insurance adjuster and I had to meet four times at the burned-out house, while he made me itemize every item we had lost. This was a daunting and really impossible task. However, he was not insensitive. He gave us a pair of twin beds that his own children had outgrown.

As the house frame began to dry out, the stairs showed signs of crumbling, and the building commissioner condemned the structure. We had thirty days to get the whole thing torn down and hauled away. Since the house was totaled, we received the entire $10,000 from the insurance, plus thirty days in the motel, including meals.

"Bobby," I said, "we won't be able to stay in a motel forever. What do you have in mind?"

"I've got it solved, Suga. The Mango house will be vacant by the end of January. I know it is much too small, but your dad is going to help me close in the carport, for starters." When the renters heard of our loss, they vacated early. Bob's home **was** small, with only two bedrooms and one bath. We began remodeling it to accommodate all of us. We added a master suite and private living room for us on one side, a dormitory and bath for the five boys, and a second dorm and bath for the five girls. We let them choose their own wallpaper, so they had their input.

Bob's original living room now held two long sofas and a ping pong table. The kitchen, with a breakfast bar for a divider, was opened to the long dining room that had previously been the carport. Bob built a fourteen-foot-long table by putting trestles under two solid-core doors. He built benches for the sides, and we used armchairs at each end. It was not fancy, but it was serviceable.

I immediately hung up a sign and got my dressmaking business going again. Bob no longer worked at the marina, as we now lived fifty miles away. He landed a position with Hugo

Schmidt, who owned a lumber yard on Hwy 60. He would be working with wood, doing what he loved.

Our new circumstances made me even more sensitive to our financial situation. Bob and I had many more discussions about his misuse of money. He was seemingly unwilling, or unable, to tell the truth. Continually, I threatened to divorce him if he did it again, but it was still only a threat. I was losing patience, however, as he undermined my every effort to manage our funds.

Of course, with a household the size of ours, there were many bumps in our road. In the interest of family harmony, we instituted a court system to handle all disagreements. The long table served as a court room. If any child had a grievance, he or she selected someone to serve as their counsel; the accused also had a representative acting as defense attorney. The jury was composed of the remaining six kids who took their places on the benches facing each other. Bob was the judge and I became the sergeant at arms, each of us seated in our armchairs at the ends of the table.

The added benefit was that they learned how the judicial system worked and what a nuisance it was to go through all that. They quickly determined what issues were worth arguing about and what was trivial enough to be overlooked or forgiven, like name calling, for instance. Under no circumstances did we allow them to call each other unkind names. So, the kids substituted funny names. I once heard Jane call Danny a "salad" and Jeff told Missy she was a "green banana," and joviality won out.

We also now had a new attitude toward material things, which would never be important to any of us again. With the generosity of friends and neighbors, little by little we furnished the new house and found a way to laugh again.

Our children were growing up and we all took great amusement in witnessing the boys' voices change. They laughed at each other as they squeaked, first Danny, then Pat. Eddie eventually lost his falsetto tone, which was missed when we sang "Twelve Days of Christmas." He had always enchanted us with "five golden rings," sounding like a choir boy. Leslie stepped up to take over that line. Peter was not far behind, then Jeffrey. The

DuMouchel boys all developed deeply resonant, baritone voices like their father. Most evenings we were treated to 'performances' as each of the boys tended to sing in the shower in their individual, beautiful tones.

Change among the girls was not so obvious. Kathy was the first to require a bra, to the envy of her little sisters. Jane, Missy and Suzi earned their bras slowly, while Leslie remained so flat-chested that Bob made a sign for her to hang around her neck that read "Front." She wore it in good humor. Nonetheless, Leslie was pretty and popular, and was the first to have a young man invite her to a cotillion.

We were often asked questions about how we managed. People wanted to know, "What do you feed all those children?" Obviously, a lot of anything. We bought pots and pans from a restaurant supply house, nothing else would do to cook three meals a day for up to thirteen people, when Steve was with us, between jobs and girlfriends. When we lived and worked at South Seas Plantation, the whole family was treated to festive meals in the dining room at Thanksgiving, Christmas and Easter, so I had not done much holiday cooking. Now we had in-laws and a grandchild, so we all pitched in to feed fifteen, plus four grandparents, when they were available.

Speaking of grandparents, we considered the possibility that any two of these young people could fall in love. Pat and Leslie appeared to be very fond of each other, who knew where that would go. Same with Kathy and Eddie, if they wanted to marry, there would be no impediments. The only drawback was that their children would only have one set of grandparents, only their father and me.

Years later, Jeff asked Missy to go out with him, but, as far as I know, only once. "Are you crazy, bro?" she insisted, "I've seen you in your underwear all my life!"

Chapter 24

Word of our fire reached Sanibel and Captiva, possibly through the post mistress, who knew everyone. We were sent money, boxes of shoes, bags of clothing and a plethora of household goods. There was an ongoing stream of generosity, from previous neighbors, as well as strangers.

An unexpected offer came from a friend who was caretaker of an enormous house on Captiva. He had communicated with the owner, now elderly and retired up north, and he invited us to use it for the entire summer. Bob couldn't leave but encouraged us to go as soon as school let out. I agonized over this, not sure I could trust him. But he assured me he would put his paychecks in the bank and I had our mail forwarded so that I could continue to pay the bills from the island. Grace offered to come with me to help look after the kids. It didn't take the children and me long to make up our minds. So, when summer arrived, we headed back to the island in two cars loaded with food, beach gear, books and games, and my portable typewriter.

Grace soon put the children to work gathering shells that washed up on the beach in the millions, paying them handsomely. With her talented hands, she fashioned the shells into clever little characters, flowers, whatnots and baskets. She called them "Sea Lovelies" and they became a hit in the island gift shops.

I busied myself with my notes, writing stories about the children. I talked to Bob twice a week from a pay phone at the Dairy Queen, always at night since he was working days. He seemed upbeat and assured me that all was going well on the home front.

Since his birthday was coming up, I decided to go home to surprise him. He was surprised, all right, and very unhappy with me for showing up unannounced. The man I found was not my Bobby. He had let his hair and beard grow for six weeks. He was dirty, unkempt, and had lost a good bit of weight. Finally, he confessed that he had just quit going to work, without notice or even a phone call. Apparently, the absence of his family had been enough to throw him into a serious depression. None of our phone conversations had offered a clue to this! I was at my wit's end. I suggested he return to the island with me, but he refused, just wanting to remain home alone.

I made an appointment to see Hugo Schmidt and asked if something had happened on the job. This soft spoken and patient man convinced me that Bob had done a fine job constructing pre-hung doors, was well liked and seemed happy until one day he simply disappeared. Schmidt's secretary had attempted to call Bob for two weeks, but the phone was never answered. Mr. Schmidt offered to let him come back to work, but when I suggested it to Bob, he was embarrassed and said that he couldn't face him again.

Desperate, with nowhere to turn and no paycheck coming in, I called my friends in The Mariner Group on Captiva and asked if they had a job for him. They were delighted. Alan Ten Broek offered him the bar manager's position, and asked if we would all come back, saying the DuMouchels had become a legend on The Plantation. I cried with relief.

While Bob seemed pleased with the offer, he wasn't overly enthusiastic. He agreed to return with me, but only to discuss it with Alan. I cut his hair, he showered and shaved, and we headed back. Ten Broek convinced him to return to his former position and we decided the children and I would return to Mango for the school year. In return, he promised to come home every two weeks and to be honest with me if he was having any problems. I begged him to help me keep our relationship intact, though it was in serious jeopardy, and we both knew it. I was optimistic that the activity at the bar would keep him from slipping into a blue funk again.

In addition to dealing with Bob, Jeff and Eddie had issues that required my attention. Jeff had run away once and when the police found him in Alabama, we decided he needed some special attention.

Eddie, on the other hand, had gone through a shoplifting phase which caused him to lose his good standing with the Boy Scouts. The previous year he had begun acting out against Bob, claiming at school that his stepfather had beaten him with a two-by-four. The truth, Bob had swatted him on the rear (through his jeans), with a flimsy little strip of quarter-round molding. Being called in to the guidance counselor's office to account for ourselves was the last straw in a series of incidents. We had debated the issue for too long and the time had come to do something.

I consulted a psychiatrist friend and was advised to give the two boys each a year or two at boarding schools, preferably not together. Thanks to a hardship reduced tuition, we were able to enroll Jeff at Mary Help of Christians, a boys' boarding school near Tampa, run by an order of Salesian brothers. A similar tuition reduction allowed Eddie to attend Frederick Military academy in Maryland. I had to take care of getting them both outfitted, registered, and delivered to their new schools.

By the Christmas holidays, things seemed to be on the upswing. We inherited a puppy from my parents, I knitted caps and mittens for the family, and Bob bought me a banjo, which I was ready for, having mastered the ukulele and guitar. He jokingly painted "Mama's Mink" on the head of the banjo, and I was thrilled. Jeff and Eddie came home for the holidays, demonstrating great progress. Both went back to their respective schools with a better attitude.

Then, out of the blue, my ex-husband, who had relocated to Ypsilanti, Michigan, with second wife Cindy, was asking if our girls could come to Michigan to live with them. He reminded me that I had had them for the last seven years. Plus, he rationalized, I was burdened with Bob being away and he would be helping me by taking the girls.

At that time, Jane was a senior at Brandon High, and not at all interested in moving to Michigan. I asked Leslie, Missy and Suzi (ages 15, 14, and 12, respectively) what they thought about living where it snowed, and the next thing I knew they were looking at gloves and coats, ice skates and sleds, in the Sears catalog. Leslie was smart enough to consult the encyclopedia and share what she learned about Michigan with her sisters. Naturally, they were all hesitant, citing that Jim was practically a stranger. The youngest two were having a hard time remembering him at all. With no pressure from me, they decided to give it a try. I had my reservations, but agreed, on the condition that he would send them back to Florida if they were unhappy. I asked him not to do anything legal, just let them visit for one school year and we'd see how they liked it. He agreed and sent them plane tickets.

What he didn't tell me, was that Cindy was pregnant with her second set of twins and expected the girls to take over housekeeping and meals, care for their four-year-old plus her older twins, who were Suzi's age. Cindy's persona was such that she wanted no competition or interference from me, so she agreed that I could write letters, but I was not to call the house. Cindy introduced all three girls to her Mormon faith and encouraged them to join activities with the Latter-Day Saints youth group, which they did.

I drove up for Leslie's high school graduation, staying in a motel. That's when I learned that soon after the girls had arrived, Jim had been put out of the house. He had been staying on the road or sleeping in his office since then. Leslie was working for a photographer part time, so I took Missy and Suzi for a little side trip to Frankenmuth, where the three of us camped out and sailed on Lake Michigan. I gave them the option of staying, but they both decided to come back to Florida. Leslie subsequently moved out of Cindy's house and went to live with one of her teachers. As a Mormon, she could receive reduced tuition to attend Brigham Young University and was planning to do so in the fall.

Chapter 25

In September 1972, word came from my Aunt Cyril that my grandmother had died. I asked Germaine to accompany me to New Orleans, but she refused. She was frightfully thin, severely addicted to alcohol, and I'm sure she didn't want her sisters to see her like that. Dad paid for my airfare and Aunt Cyril and her husband met me at the airport.

We gathered at Schoen Funeral home on Canal Street, following a lengthy wake the previous night. Uncle Lee had brought my grandfather from the nursing home, without informing him of his wife's death. Uncle Donald told the waiting relatives that he was going to escort him into a private room to explain why they were all there and invited his siblings to join him. When I rose from my chair, Donald and his wife, Polly, attempted to keep me out of the room. "Not you, Lynne," Polly said, "just the family."

Just the family? But, wasn't I family? I was shocked. Having been raised by the senior Sarrats, I never dreamed I would not be included. Unexpectedly, my grandfather reached for my hand, and with tears in his eyes, he said, "You stay with me, baby, they're going to tell me something bad." He had me by the wrist and didn't release his grip as we walked solemnly into the private room. He then pulled me down to sit next to him on a loveseat, taking my hand in both of his while of his children stood silently and Donald told him that his beloved wife was gone. Père cried and kept me by his side for the rest of the service, not releasing his grip on my hand until they ushered him into a waiting limo for the drive to the cemetery. Being with him again brought back so many memories, particularly years of his generosity, patience and gentleness.

Mignon and Pierre Sarrat
50th Anniversary

On the flight home, I recalled when, at the age of twelve, Mère and Père were eager to educate me regarding both family history and the culture of their beloved New Orleans. They took me to Chalmette, where the Battle of New Orleans took place, then up and down the River Road where they pointed out plantations and told tales of interesting people and things that happened there. The stories and characters, so rich and colorful, it all sounded like a movie script. They related history about the French and Spanish people, the Creoles, who created a small piece of Europe there along the bayous.

"And what did you and your brother, Uncle George, do when you were boys, Père?" I asked on one excursion.

"We were tutored up to sixth grade." he said, "We read the classics and studied Latin and English, in addition to our native Creole languages of Spanish and French. Our mother taught us to dance, plus manners and other refinements.

There were no organized sports, but we learned to hunt, fish, row and fence. We trained our horses and we loved to go to the races. We had black playmates on our home place, mulattos, and at Christmas we gave gifts to them and the cane cutters. George liked to gamble, and I liked the theater.

When I was of age, I was apprenticed to a jewelry designer before joining the New Orleans Cotton Exchange. George wanted to study abroad but international relations had been shaky since World War I and it wasn't considered safe. We enjoyed drinking in the quarter, along with our cousins, and gambling at the Elkin Club. And, of course, we attended balls in the homes of our friends. Men in the business of merchandising and ordinary trade were considered plebeian and excluded from these aristocratic clubs and social events."

"You and Uncle George owned your own horses, Père?" I asked, amazed.

"Yes, girlie, practically everyone did, and carriages, too. Our horses didn't have shoes, because we only rode on dirt roads, muddy roads, to be precise. We raced them informally along the bayou, all the way to Lake Pontchartrain."

Père went on to explain that back then the levee leaked and much of the city was muddy. There were no sidewalks, so pedestrians walked on planks, with little bridges at the end of every block used to cross the street. Since the city sits below sea level there was no way to drain the water away.

He said that this water also held rats, water moccasins and even alligators which moved about freely in ditches. But, he said, the most lethal nuisance was the mosquitoes. Their stings carried deadly Yellow Fever. People slept under huge lengths of mosquito netting, called 'baire', to avoid their sting.

"Did your family get the fever?" I asked.

"Thank God, no. They left the city when it got dangerous each year and lived in their summer homes on the Gulf coast."

"What about the poor people who didn't have two houses?" I fretted.

"They remained, and many of them died, particularly in the first few years."

"If conditions were so terrible, why did people stay here?" I questioned.

"They were colonists, my dear, most from Spain and France, a few from Britain, Germany and Italy. They were brave people venturing into a place of opportunity known back then as "the Indies". One of my ancestors had a hand in settling the colony, with French Canadian naval officer, Jean-Baptiste LeMoyne Bienville, who became the first governor. According to the census, the colony was half French, a quarter Spanish, and the rest a mixture of native Americans and various Europeans. The French chevaliers and Spanish dons governed Louisiana."

"What else would you like to know?" he asked, encouraged by my curiosity.

"Tell me, why are some of the streets paved with bricks?" I asked.

"That came about in my day. Because the territory was swamp land, with no stone of its own, the streets were paved with Belgian bricks that arrived as ballast on European ships."

He pointed out lamp posts installed in 1796 that originally illuminated only ten paces in the French Quarter, and were now replaced by proper lights, both ornate and functional.

They took me for afternoon tea at the Napoleon House after walking around looking at the statue of President Jackson on horseback, in front of the cathedral. Père said that General Jackson brought 1500 of his Tennessee volunteer troops down to Natchez to successfully defend the territory against the British.

Père explained, "What we know as the Vieux Carre was once called the Place d'Armes, a parade ground. It was useless because it was a flooded mud hole bordered by the Presbytere, St. Louis Cathedral and the Cabildo, plus stables and a jail. The Cabildo was the seat of government. The red brick Pontalba buildings on both sides were built by Baroness Micaela Pontalba, whose bloodlines were the same as mine. Her initials are designed in grillwork on the balconies. And note, the river completes the fourth side of the square."

When I was jolted from my reverie, I reflected on what I had just experienced when we said goodbye to Mère. What would I tell my children of their great grandmother? She had been hard on me at first, but benevolent, too. She had been angry with my mother, not me. It was, in my opinion, important for them to know we should appreciate all that is done for us. I wanted them to know I was grateful to her and I promised myself I would travel again to New Orleans to see my beloved grandfather, my Père.

Our pilot reminded us about seat belts and tray tables, and as the wheels touched down in Tampa, I was happy to be home.

Chapter 26

One of our favorite TV quiz shows was "What's My Line." This had been a popular CBS show from 1950-1967 hosted by John Daly. It involved contestants being questioned by a panel of celebrities to determine their occupation. When the show was revived for the 1972-73 season, with Larry Blyden as the host, I took a bold chance and wrote them a letter. I had taken an interesting job with Gradiaz Annis, one of the old respected cigar producers in Ybor City. Cigar smokers from all over the world came to watch the elderly Cuban men and women hand-roll the cigars. I was the token white American who greeted them at the factory and led them on a tour while detailing the history and culture that produced their fine cigars.

When the producers read that I sold cigars and was the mother of twelve children, they accepted me. I received an invite to appear on the show, roundtrip airline tickets to New York city, and a room at the Plaza Hotel.

My employer was delighted to have the publicity and provided an escort from their New York office, a young lady named Carol Whey. She gave me a tour of the home office, where I saw several executives whom I had met when they visited Tampa.

After a lovely dinner, Carol and I saw the Broadway production of "Irene." This included backstage access after the final curtain, where I met Debbie Reynolds. She was charming and spent a lot of time with us. My evening was topped off with a horse-drawn carriage ride around Central Park.

The next morning, I was on my own to find 30 Rockefeller Center and the NBC Studio. Stepping out on the sidewalk, I was overwhelmed by the traffic. I hailed a taxi and told the driver where I wanted to go, but he refused to take me the two blocks to the studio because it was in the opposite direction! He advised me, at the top of his lungs to get out, cross the street and walk. Learning it was so close, I crossed the wildly busy street and enjoyed the walk and the fair, sunny morning. It had been fifteen years since I had worked in New York for AT&T, many blocks closer to the Battery. Apparently, I had forgotten the protocol.

Upon entering the glass-enclosed reception area, I gave the receptionist my name and was given a one-page script, the last line of which ended with, "Alan Alda guesses cigars."

"Really?" I asked. "How do we know he'll get it?"

"Just please take a seat in the next room," she dismissed me politely. A second girl appeared and ushered me into a large, brightly lit room where I took a seat among the guests for the five shows that would be taped that day.

The panel consisted of Arlene Francis, Alan Alda, Soupy Sales, and Meredith MacRae (Gordon and Sheila MacRae's daughter). Gradiaz Annis had been given this information in advance and provided me handsome wooden gift boxes of cigars with the names of the panelists imprinted on each wrapper. I met Blyden and asked him to stash the four boxes in his desk. The four celebrity challengers, Sheila MacRae, John Cassavetes, James Brolin, and Robert Alda (Alan's father) were also there as taping began. When we had some downtime and could talk among ourselves, Cassavetes entertained me with a brief exercise, demonstrating how much more each of us sees than we realize.

Everything moved along, as we were called up one at a time to tape the eighteen minutes of a half-hour show. I was the last contestant before the lunch break and I was confident that I had handled my session well. I took the gift boxes from Blyden and handed out the personalized cigars to the panel members on my way off stage. They were all receptive and courteous until I handed the final box to Alan Alda. He refused it and made a scene, acting outraged, saying in a stadium voice, he would not have cigars in his house!

Soupy said quietly, "Just take them, Alan." But, snatching the box rudely from me, Alda slammed it into Sales' chest, saying "You take the dirty things!" Soupy, holding both boxes, tried to apologize for Alda's behavior as I made my way off the set, completely humiliated. I feared I had just lost my job.

Lovely Arlene Francis came right to me as the taping ended, apologizing for Alda, saying, "He's always been a spoiled brat, just ignore him," and asked if I would walk out with her to grab some lunch, which I did. She thanked me profusely for the cigars, saying, "My husband, Martin, will be so jealous next time we have a dinner party and I hand out my personal cigars!" We grabbed hot dogs and a quick cup of coffee from street vendors as we headed to Saks Fifth Avenue to shop for an umbrella she wanted. I thanked her for her kindness and went back to the Plaza while she headed back to tape the afternoon segments.

Before heading home, I made a short detour, by train, to visit neighborhood friends from Mobile, who lived in Westminster, Maryland. The husband, Al Williams, was an engineer at Random House. I told him about the book I had been writing and he offered to have his secretary type my manuscript and said he would submit it "over the transom", as they say in publishing circles.

As a result of his efforts, there was some interest in the book and I was beginning to believe it might get published. Then he called me later to tell me of a delay; it seems the Watergate affair had just hit the news and all five major publishers immediately planned to feature it. Their current list would be pushed back to a future season. I was offered a shift to Doubleday, but with no agent representing me through some legal brouhaha, the book became mired in red tape and I couldn't even get the manuscript back.

On a whim, some months later, I asked one of my friends in New York to go to Doubleday and just ask for my little manuscript. They located it and she read over it, made a few corrections and suggestions, and sent it to me. When it was in my hands again, since I am by nature an artist, I decided to begin a comic strip instead of a book about the kids. With not much free time, I did a bit of work on it, but it remained in limbo for ten years, a silly dream on the shelf.

Once home again, I taught Jane the exercise Cassavetes had taught me, and she used it for a speech competition at school. The trick was to have your audience remain focused on the speaker, and without turning or even moving their eyes, they are able to answer many questions about things they don't even realize are within their consciousness. We take knowledge for granted without registering it. For instance, the time of day, season of the year, people nearby, the weather outside, identifying sounds you don't even realize you're hearing. Jane practiced until she became thoroughly skilled on the subject and delivered her presentation with aplomb. The judges were impressed, awarding her a trophy so large she could hardly carry it home.

While she was telling me and the younger kids about her success, a special delivery interrupted us. I had to sign for a letter addressed to "Mr. Robert DuMouchel," then I let her conclude, as her excitement was contagious.

That night I presented the letter to Bob, bringing a totally unexpected tirade from him. "Don't EVER sign for anything, especially if it's addressed to me!" he bellowed, in a surprisingly uncharacteristic manner. Tearing the unopened letter to bits, he stormed out of the room.

I rescued enough of the envelope from the trash to ascertain it was from Stowers Funeral Home, and I assumed it was an advertisement. Why did he explode over that, I wondered? When he calmed down, I asked.

"Not your problem, Suga," he said, "I still owe Stowers for June's funeral, that's all. I hate bill collectors! When they call, I usually hold the phone by the cord, dangle the receiver in a metal trash can, and rattle it against the sides until they hang up!"

I was stunned, June had died over three years before. How and why had he kept this from me? What else didn't I know? The next day, while he was at work, I called Dick Stowers and apologized. He and I agreed to a monthly payment to clear the debt. Bob and I never discussed Stowers again. But I decided I needed to be more diligent in monitoring our checkbook and credit cards. I had lost a little more faith in my husband.

Chapter 27

With Bob at South Seas, I had much to do, not the least of which was ridding the house of June's ghost. We had ample evidence that she was still there, haunting us.

I was sitting at the breakfast bar sipping iced coffee one afternoon before the kids came home, when an upper corner cabinet door slowly creaked open. I looked up, curious. A wedge of light fell on the oversized pressure cooker in the back of the storage cache behind four pint-size cans, half-filled with leftover paint, plus a jar of brushes from my last project. I had always been afraid to use the cooker because my cousin had been badly burned and scarred when her mother's pressure cooker exploded! On the other hand, Bob seemed to fear nothing and used it whenever he cooked, because it would accommodate a large corned beef, a head of cabbage, plus potatoes and carrots, all at one time. I didn't even want to be in the kitchen when he cooked with it.

Before I could get off the stool to close the cabinet, the pressure cooker fell onto the terrazzo floor, making a horrendously loud noise. It had, inexplicably, fallen from the shelf without disturbing the paint cans in front of it. Despite its handle protruding off one side, the monster cooker somehow proceeded to roll around the bar to where I was sitting. Aghast, I stared as it came to rest at my feet!

I called Michael and told him about this incredible feat and he just laughed, saying I should not be drinking alone in the afternoon! Iced coffee??

Another day I was sitting on the sofa in our living room watching "As the World Turns," with some sewing in my hands, and I heard a squeaking or low scraping sound, back and forth, back and forth, like something rocking on rusty springs. Sonny Boy, our puppy, was at my feet.

"Go look, Sonny," I said to him, pointing at the open door leading to our dining room. The little blonde dog crept only to the door sill and wouldn't go any farther. Whimpering, he just stopped there. I prompted again, "Go see, Sonny! See if somebody came in the front." But when the pup just cowered down on his belly, I put down my sewing and went to see for myself. In the low light, I glimpsed something blue that seemed to blow upward, as in a puff of smoke. The squeaking stopped abruptly. I turned the light on and there was nothing unusual, only the dining table, benches and end chairs. But the poor little dog was afraid to follow me into that room! I checked the closure on the door at the front of what used to be the carport, to assure that it was locked, then went back to my sewing.

The next time I talked with Bob I related these two incidents, and he said he had no answer for the pressure cooker's performance. However, his father had given June an old, overstuffed, squeaky chair that she kept on the carport. He said she spent hours rocking out there, watching the kids play on the vacant lot next door. I was stunned when he described the noise the rocker made, but even more shocked when I learned that June constantly wore a blue housecoat in the daytime! Was that the puff of blue I clearly saw?

I had known June well before she died, we had laughed together more than once. She would not have hurt me when she was living, she certainly wasn't going to hurt me from the grave. I decided not to bring this up in front of the children yet.

Pat came home from school one afternoon and was surprised by the sound of my electric typewriter. My car was gone, so he assumed I was at work. He approached my bedroom door and knocked. He waited, knocked again, and then getting no response, he gingerly opened the door. The room was empty, the typewriter off, so he closed the door, perplexed. The typing resumed twice more. He looked in, once again checking my typewriter, but it was definitely off. At dinner that night he told Peter, Kathy, Jane, and me, but we had no explanation.

Another day, alone in the kitchen, I was startled to hear the unmistakable sounds of a ping pong match. Opening the door, I glimpsed the two paddles on the table, one resting on a ball. I went back to cooking but had to look again when I heard the same activity. Could Pat and Peter be playing tricks on me, I wondered? Is this some trick of Jane's? But they were at school! Nobody was here except Sonny Boy and me.

"Mom!" Pat said when I told them, "I think we have a ghost!"

When I told Bob, he just whistled. "What's that supposed to mean?" I inquired.

"It's June!" he nearly shouted over the phone. "On four different bases, while we were traipsing all over the globe, June was always the best ping pong player in the N.C.O. clubs!"

"And did she have a typewriter?" I had to ask.

"No," he said, "she never owned one, but everywhere we were stationed she worked as a court stenographer!"

I consulted a woman with knowledge of the paranormal. "This is not so uncommon," the mystic woman said to me. "All you need is for someone to communicate with her and tell her to move on." Communicate?

That opportunity came from an unexpected source. I had received an offer from another large combined family who wanted to buy the Mango house with its two oversized dormitories. We agreed to move out when the Brandon house became available at the end of March.

About six months after the Donnelly's moved in, along with the monthly payment, I received a note that said:

"Dear Suga,

*Enclosed please find my check in the amount of $350
for September. Please come see us when you're in
the area.*

Sincerely, Joyce.

*P.S. We have a ghost! He follows my daughter, Joy,
all around!"*

I had to call and tell her the ghost was not a man, but Bob's first wife, June, and she was harmless. She then informed me that they had had been trying to communicate with their ghost with a Ouija board. I considered Ouija a child's toy, but finally agreed to bring some of our children over to participate. They were fascinated by the whole idea.

As each one of Joy's children sat opposite one of our children and held the wooden planchette, it moved all over the board and answered their questions. Both Joyce and I watched with a jaundiced eye. They asked if June was in heaven, and the answer was, "not yet"; they asked if Jesus was there, and the reply was "just like all the rest." I suggested they ask what my grandfather's name was, which June wouldn't have known, and the answer was, "AGT". Correct, but the older kids knew that.

At that moment Steve showed up and the planchette flew out of two players' hands and crashed against the wall! They tried again, and it happened again, so they changed players and questions. What became obvious was that as long as Steve was in the room, "June" wouldn't cooperate. "I'll leave," Steve offered. "My mother and I had an argument the last time I saw her, and I didn't even come home when she died. I guess she's still mad at me."

Of course, nothing was resolved, but it was a fun evening. The kids enjoyed seeing their old home with new people living in it. And when Bobby and I talked next, he was amused when I told him about the whole "ghost" thing. He said he'd be coming home Sunday.

Chapter 28

After Sunday mass, I was preparing a homecoming meal for Bob, when I received a phone call from a state trooper. Asking if I was Mrs. DuMouchel, he informed me that Bob had been in a serious accident on the road near Arcadia.

"Is he alive?" I cried, desperately.

"I'm not at the scene, ma'am, I couldn't say. I was just instructed to make the call."

On the way there, imagining the worst, I offered God a bargain. If Bobby was still alive, I would give up my banjo that I had yearned for. He was admitted to MacDill AFB Hospital. The same hospital to which he had made his wild dash in 1968, trying to save June. He had a severely mangled leg; I was just relieved that he was alive. A deal was a deal and the banjo would be sold.

I went to see him every day and took the children for evening and weekend visits. Jeff was hoping to see "blood and guts," but settled for a lot of gauze, once he saw his dad was smiling.

A week passed, then two, and still they had not set his leg. I was livid, arguing with every doctor who would listen, but all I got were excuses and delays. Finally, I was told by a remorseful doctor, "Sorry ma'am, but we have to take care of active-duty personnel first, and then we can attend to the retirees. We are simply understaffed." There was no use arguing.

I had to get Bobby moved to a hospital where he would receive the care he needed. I called Dick Stowers, in Brandon, and asked if he could send one of his vehicles to transport Bob to St. Joseph's Hospital in Tampa. He arrived safe and sound and the doctors set his leg that night. It was going to be a long recovery, and the two-week delay at MacDill hadn't helped. At one point, he was told that he might lose the leg and would require extensive therapy.

As the weeks turned into months, Bob's trips back to Mac-Dill grew shorter. It became easier on me after the large cast was removed and he could drive again. His attitude was better, my old Bobby, and that kept me going.

After his recovery, he walked funky, but then, since I had known him, he always had. This was just a different limp. When I had time, I got him up to dance at home, and this kept him cheerful. Having ice skated as a kid in Michigan, I never could break him of wanting to use skating moves on the dance floor. "What's really important?" Missy used to say, "Just keep'em laughing."

By the time he was ready to go back to work, eighteen months later, The Mariner Group was preparing to open Greenlefe Golf and Tennis Resort, a community near Haines City. They offered him the temporary manager's position while they attempted to fill it permanently. We hurriedly set out to buy him a tuxedo and two new sport coats to pump up his wardrobe.

A lovely perk with this job was a flight for me to the site on their private plane every two weeks. With no preschoolers any longer, I was free to get away to visit this beautiful, elegant community. Every weekend spent there was a luxurious mini-honeymoon!

The high point for me at Greenlefe was the first New Years' Eve dance. Right after Christmas, I packed up the new evening gown I had designed and headed off to dine and dance with the man-in-charge, my handsome husband, as we welcomed in the New Year.

Six months later, the bubble burst. Bob came home, telling me they had hired the permanent manager and didn't need him any longer. He said it was just as well, because he needed to be closer to MacDill in order for the doctors there to finally perform some critical surgery on his back. Surprised at this news, I asked what the doctors had told him.

"They said it's my war injury actin' up. If I don't get this surgery, I may lose my ability to walk." He explained.

"Bobby, you haven't complained of back pain to me and I'm not sure I trust the doctors at MacDill. What's the name of the doctor?"

"Oh, you can't call him," he said with finality. "They won't let you talk to the doctors, only a patient can get through to them."

"Bob, be serious. I'm your wife, your next of kin," I insisted.

"Listen, Suga, the next time I see the spinal specialist I'll ask him for a detailed description of my problem, in writing. It's very severe, but he's monitoring my condition to see how it develops."

He asked for $150 for a back brace and, as usual, I gave it to him. I was extremely busy, and although I was not convinced by his explanation, I accepted his word. With my front desk job in Tampa, sewing all hours and a newspaper column I had picked up in Clair Mel, I had neither the time nor the energy to check up on him. I, once again, reiterated that if he wasn't telling me the truth, I was through.

Keeping himself occupied with small chores around the house, Bob puttered in the kitchen and stayed active, driving himself over sixty miles each way every month to see his doctors at the military base. He reported that the doctor had determined he was definitely going to undergo back surgery, but he was on a waiting list and would be called when the time was right. Needless to say, I never did get a written description of his issue.

Meanwhile, Eddie had been causing problems at the military academy. It wasn't a good fit for him, to say the least. He constantly broke curfew and violated his privileges in every way possible. The final straw came when he and a friend were caught selling fire arms in the nearby community! They had spirited guns from the armory, piece by piece, concealing the parts in their book bags or jackets. I received a call from the commander notifying me that Eddie was being expelled immediately and would be sent home. I was over my head at the time and couldn't handle another crisis. So, I called Jim, begging him to retrieve Eddie and take him into his home. He agreed, on the condition that there was to be no communication between my son and myself. Jim was back with Cindy, and she had agreed to taking Eddie, under protest. This was her caveat.

His stay with them, predictably, didn't last long. He had boldly offered Cindy a joint and she threw him out while Jim was on the road. After months of living on the streets, Eddie and a friend stole a car, intending to reach Florida, but they ended up in juvenile detention. Jim was called to court but couldn't take him home a second time; Cindy had forbidden it. He claimed he had no choice but to consent to our son being sent to a reform school.

All of this passed, without a single phone call to me. When I was finally brought up to date, I had no alternative, but to wait for his release at the age of eighteen.

Chapter 29

As time went on, Bob's cough only got worse. He was diagnosed with emphysema but still refused to give up cigarettes. I decided to take a day off to accompany him to MacDill, planning to discuss both his smoking and his upcoming back surgery with his doctor. I took along a book and read while he was in the examining room. When an hour had elapsed, and he hadn't returned, I approached the receptionist and asked if she knew the status of Sgt. DuMouchel's scheduled surgery.

She frowned quizzically and checked his file. "There's no surgery planned, Mrs. DuMouchel, the Sarge is in for a routine checkup. It's part of his retirement privilege."

"Are you sure?" I asked, dumbfounded.

"Yes, I'm sure."

Neurotransmitters went into overdrive, dumping a load of chemicals into my bloodstream. "Please tell Sgt. DuMouchel when he comes out," I said coldly, "that I'll be waiting in the car."

As he settled into the passenger seat, I very calmly asked, with extra gravitas, "Why did you do this, Bobby?" He knew exactly what I was asking.

"I was trying to buy time. I knew our marriage was in trouble, but that if I needed care, you would stay with me."

He then revealed that he had been fired from Greenlefe! He had helped himself to a few dollars from the register. When the bookkeeper confronted him, in front of guests, Bob punched him in the face and knocked him out. He was lucky he hadn't been arrested.

My brain couldn't comprehend what he had done, and that he, once again, had compounded it by lying. I was flat out of sympathy. I drove home, saying nothing more. My head was splitting. I knew what I had to do. When we arrived, I went inside, packed his suitcase, put some towels and bed linens in a plastic garbage bag, and added his cigarettes from the freezer. Amazed at being able to hold it together, I then made a phone call to an apartment complex and rented him a small flat. I charged to my credit card, since he had none. Swallowing the vitriol, I went to confront him. He was in the living room, watching TV. This is how you do the really hard things, you put one foot in front of the other. Keeping my voice level and my broken heart under control, I simply said, "Come with me, please, Bobby."

He watched me place the suitcase and the bag full of linens in the car. "We're going to the grocery store," I said with a determination that I didn't feel, "then I'm taking you to Ybor City, to your new apartment."

"I guess I deserve this," he said in a calm voice, as I backed the car out and headed to town.

"You brought it on yourself," I said sadly.

Later, he asked Mike to help him pick up his car from my house. I don't know how he explained the situation to his children. By that time, the only DuMouchels still at home were Kathy and Jeffrey. There was a good chance that the older children had been expecting this for a long time.

I looked in on him after a few weeks, and he was not unhappy, nor did he complain. He laughed as he told me about setting fire to his mattress while smoking in bed, then getting locked out in his underwear when he stepped out to retrieve his paper.

Sometimes peace and harmony come with a price. I would no longer have his strong arms around me or laugh at his silly jokes. He had made me feel like a woman. I had felt cherished. Was it ever real?

And although my friends considered me cold, I stuck to my word. Steve and Kari, his wife, came with me to my divorce lawyer. I never dreamed it would end like this, but by May 3, 1976, it was over.

Chapter 30

I am struck by the uncanny similarities between my life at that moment and my predicament earlier when Jim divorced me. Déjà vu! There I was again with a house full of children, a mortgage, odd jobs that didn't add up to enough income, and an ex-husband, upon whom I could not rely. Given, he wasn't a cheat, but he was a liar. They had that in common.

At the same time, there were differences. I was no longer a frightened, unworldly girl. I had been through a great deal in those seven years. I now realized that I had the smarts and the tenacity to survive. I had come out on the other side a mature woman with a more realistic view of the world. I had experienced what I still believed was true love and had felt cherished and protected; something that was lacking the first time around. I now had seven children to provide for, rather than six, but they were older and more independent. And I had an additional five children who would prove to be a great source of encouragement and support. I had friendships and a community base which I sorely lacked when Jim and I were moving from state to state on a regular basis.

The one thing that had never changed, the rock upon which my life was built – my faith. I still invoked the Blessed Mother in my times of need and doubt. I was still a good Catholic girl who took comfort in the belief that there was someone looking over me.

So, what's next? I put one foot in front of the other and continue my journey. I needed to assure the children that we would be fine. I needed to decide whether we would stay in Brandon. I needed a full-time job, a career. Help me, Blessed Mother!

DON'T MISS THE NEXT INSTALLMENT IN THE SERIES!

The French Resolution

Lynne's third book tells of grief over the loss of a child and her husband and provides an end to her quest to discover the identity of her parents. Readers are provided a look into her reign as Queen of Mardi Gras and a surprise visitor reveals how the kids managed to melt her license plate without damaging the car!

There is talk of a fourth book!

An unwanted child, nick-named Suga, is abandoned in New Orleans. Her story offers a glimpse into the life of an overprotected child who is reminded repeatedly by her benefactor that she must be grateful because nobody wanted her. She struggles to overcome the stigma and evolves into an accomplished and beloved mother of six children.

Despite numerous challenges, including a horrendous acci-dent, a nomad lifestyle, and a husband with a wandering eye, she dusts off an old skill, learns new ones, and inspires her offspring.

"If a storyteller's skill can be ranked by how engaged the reader is, you rank high. I was hooked from the start of the book and left eagerly awaiting the continuation of your story."
            Mary K.

"Lynne has the talent to bring the reader into her story and long for more."
            Mary Ann Revell, Educator

"Refined Suga spans a lifetime of inspiration and generosity. It is truly a magical journey of unconditional love."
            Jane Kreisman Soslow, Owner of Gramps Books
            Author, Editor, Educator

76720124R00109

Made in the USA
Columbia, SC
27 September 2019